LADY IN THE SHADOW

by

Cheryl Costantino

as told to

Joanne Jacquart

Acclaimed Books

Dallas, Texas

Acclaimed Books
P.O. Box 180399
Dallas, TX 75218-0399

ISBN 0-932294-13-8
Library of Congress Catalog Card Number: 81-71112

Distributed by Acclaimed Books, Box 180399, Dallas, TX 75218-0399.

Acclaimed Books is the publishing department of International Prison Ministry founded by Chaplain Ray Hoekstra.

Printed in Belarus by Printcorp. LP # 347 of 11.05.99. 40 Staroborisovsky Trakt, Minsk, 220141. Ord. 03076C. Qty 20 000 cps.

Dedication

To my children: Lori-Ann, Tony, Rocco, and Michelle, who went through this experience with me; and to Deborah and Maranatha, who were born after.

To my husband, Frank, who patiently led me into a relationship with Jesus Christ.

Most of all to Jesus Christ, who brought our relationship from darkness into light.

And to prisoners' wives everywhere, this book is for *you*!

Contents

LADY
IN THE
SHADOW

Chapter 1

A burst of gunfire, like a shootout in a western movie, exploded outside my apartment. The crack of each weapon followed on top of the report of another – a rapid-fire succession of sharp, shrill explosions, as if someone had set off a string of firecrackers outside the front door.

I sat frozen in my chair, unable to move. Gunshots. Here, at my apartment. I knew my husband, Frank, was in the middle of it. I knew it as surely as I know my own reflection in a mirror.

It was Saturday night and Frank had gone out somewhere. I had felt uneasy ever since he left. It was a combination of little insignificant things; the way he acted at supper, the way he snapped at our two children, Tony and Lori, the way he picked at his food and kept glancing at the clock. I knew something was wrong, but I didn't know what. He was always so secretive about everything.

After he left I tried to relax and settled into a chair near the window. I was eight months pregnant with our third child and found it difficult to get into a comfortable position. It had been a clear, sunny day. The evening was warm and pleasant. The breeze brought a fresh spring fragrance to the air that came softly through the open window.

It was 8 p.m. and our children were asleep in their

bedroom. I was in the living room with Pat and her live-in boyfriend, Johnny "Wop." Pat and I had been close since highschool and she spent a lot of time at our place. She was tall and thin, with big blue eyes and sandy hair. Frank called her "Twiggy."

Johnny was an easygoing, popular Italian from the old country who spoke broken English. He had an endless supply of funny stories that were even funnier because of his Italian accent. His laugh was contagious. He was well built, medium height, broody with blonde hair and blue eyes. He had muscular arms, but wore long-sleeved shirts, even in the summer. The sleeves hid the needle tracks in his veins. He was a user and a small-time pusher. I accepted him even though drugs were not part of our life-style.

He had been sitting in the living room talking for a long time. But I couldn't shake my uneasiness. I knew something was wrong and I was afraid. I kept fidgeting in my chair, trying to get my body into a comfortable position. But I was edgy, anxious. I had almost convinced myself that I was making a big thing of nothing, when I looked out the window and saw Guido standing outside.

Guido was a friend of Frank's, a prominent racketeer, a man of considerable reputation in the underworld. He was tough, hard and smart. He wasn't afraid of anything or anybody. He was in his forties, a well-built, good-looking man who always dressed well. He wore a white knit sport shirt, casual pale yellow slacks and white shoes. His dark wavy hair was neatly trimmed and the slight greying at his temples completed the distinguished look. He was not the kind of guy who would be just hanging around.

I went outside and said, "Guido, are you looking for Frank? He's not here."

"Yes, I know, Bunny. Why don't you just go back inside?" He had a way of making a suggestion a command.

Johnny sensed my uneasiness and suggested we play a game of cards. I began to unwind as we talked and laughed at Johnny's latest jokes.

Then the gun battle erupted without warning. Pat ducked into Johnny's lap and then they both hit the floor. The reality of what was happening slowly penetrated my mind.

"Bunny! Get down!" Johnny yelled.

I was terrified, but I couldn't move. A numbness crept over my body, and my mouth went dry with that all-too-familiar taste of fear. My heart began racing as wave after wave of heavy dread shook my body.

Through the open window I could hear the sounds of glass shattering, bullets caroming off metal, the scrape of running footsteps across gravel in the parking lot. Men were screaming and shouting profanities.

Pat was wide-eyed as she gasped, "My god, what's happening?"

Finally, the battle ended and there was only the sound of our heavy breathing and wind blowing softly through the open window. I waited for another outbreak, but there was only silence.

I couldn't stand the suspense. I got up and headed for the door.

"Where are you going?" Johnny yelled.

"Frank's out there," I said panicking, "maybe shot. I've got to go see."

Johnny jumped up and blocked my way to the door. "Don't be stupid, Bunny," he said. "You don't know if Frank is involved in that out there. There are one hundred families living in this complex, over half of them are Cuban refugees. There's been a lot of friction with them lately. It's probably them."

"No, it's Frank. I just know it," I screamed as I reached for the door.

"Are you crazy?" he said. "What if the shooting starts up again?"

"If you won't let me go out, then you go," I said.

"I'm not going out there and get killed," he said.

"Then get out of my way," I said as I pushed past him and ran outside.

I couldn't believe the mess. It was dark out, but the light from the street lamps and the apartment windows illuminated the parking lot. The cars were all shot up, with gaping holes in the windshields and tires blown out.

Broken glass everywhere gleamed dimly in the pale light. Bullet holes riddled the apartment buildings and jagged pieces of glass glistened where the windows had been. Scraps of metal and shards of glass littered the pavement.

I frantically looked around, but didn't see any dead bodies. And I didn't see Frank. The piercing sound of sirens broke the stillness and within minutes police were swarming everywhere. I went back inside trembling. I knew that Frank had been in it. There was no other explanation. All the signs had been there. Frank's irritability, his preoccupation with time, and finally, Guido coming by confirmed it.

Pat and Johnny stayed with me until about 11 p.m. After they left, I went to bed, but I couldn't sleep. Frank came home very late that night.

"Where have you been?" I asked. "I've been worried sick."

"Out," he said.

"Who were you and Guido shooting it out with?"

"What are you talking about, Bunny?"

"I saw Guido outside just before the gunfight. Don't lie to me. I know you were out there with him."

He just shrugged it off, refused to talk about it, and said my fear was silly. Not one bit of the emotion I was feeling seemed silly to me.

Violence was part of the way we lived during the eleven years that Frank was a major criminal. Part of me enjoyed the excitement and high style of living it brought. But along with it came the fear. How many times had I wondered, when he walked out the door on "business," would he be back? Would he be arrested? Worst of all, would he be dead?

Chapter 2

There was a certain naive attraction to fast living for me. I had all the excitement that went along with it and could participate in the exhilaration Frank felt after a robbery and still remain a safe distance from the danger involved.

One night I was visiting with my friends, Carrie and Irene, whose husbands were also involved in crime. We were discussing what it must feel like to actually be a part of a robbery. There must be a certain high that came from that fear of being caught. Why else would they take the unnerving chances that they did?

We came up with the idea of planning our own robbery and not letting the guys in on it. We were usually the ones sitting home worrying about them while they were out on a robbery. Why not reverse that and let them feel what it was like? Maybe they would understand our fears a little better. As we talked about it, we liked the idea.

We decided the appropriate attire for the occasion was black – black T-shirts, black slacks, and of course, black gloves. All three of us had dark hair, so that was no problem. We agreed to meet at Carrie's the next night at dusk.

The steady drizzle of rain made it a dreary night.

After we piled into our Olds 98 we realized we didn't have a plan.

Irene had just gone through a divorce and was mad at her ex-in-laws. "Let's go to their house and steal something from them," she said. "They're loaded and they're supposed to be out of town right now."

"We could hit some other houses in their neighborhood, too," Carrie said. "They live in a wealthy section of town."

I agreed and we headed for their house. We parked the car in a nearby parking lot and I locked the doors.

"What the hell are you locking the car for?" Carrie asked. "What if we have to make a fast get-away?"

"Hey, there could be thieves around here. Frank would kill me if someone stole our car," I said.

Irene shook her head in disbelief.

We crept around to the back of the house. Everything was dark. I could feel the blood begin to race through my veins and my hands felt clammy.

"Hand me the screwdriver, Carrie," Irene whispered.

She began to try to pry open the door to the Florida room. It was a closed-in patio with jalousie windows.

Suddenly she gasped. "Someone's in the house watching television in the dark and I think he saw us!" she said in a hoarse whisper.

We panicked and took off running across the back yard. Carrie ran like a deer, kicking off her shoes as she went so she could move even faster.

Irene was right behind her and stopped to pick up the shoes. I tripped over her when she stopped and fell with a thud to the ground.

As I scrambled to my feet, Irene held up the shoes and said, "This could have been evidence to convict us."

We heard a muffled scream up ahead. Carrie had

run into the clotheslines. The drizzle turned into a downpour and we were drenched.

We scrambled across the next yard and came to a home-made fence consisting of three wires. Irene grabbed two of the wires and held them apart so we could get through. Carrie zipped right on through like a breeze, but I stepped on the top wire and got Irene tangled between them!

We finally made it to the car and my hands were shaking as I fumbled for the keys to unlock the door. We looked like three drowned rats. We laughed all the way home and Carrie called us Ding, Dong and Clunk.

When we were pulling into the parking lot at Carrie's apartment we realized the guys would never let us live this down. At least we had to arrive with some loot. So we went to a nearby port and lifted a chaise lounge.

When we walked in, Carrie's husband took one look at us and said, "Where the hell have you been?"

We glanced at each other and just said, "Out!" We weren't about to admit defeat. But neither were we interested in furthering our career in crime. I preferred participating at a safe distance and just enjoying the luxuries it bought.

But as the luxuries increased, so did the tension between Frank and me. I resented having to live through the fear of Frank being caught or killed. At times I hated him for this and wouldn't speak to him for days.

He would just take off and I wouldn't know where he was for several days. When he returned, he would say he was involved in a poker game, but I began to suspect he was seeing another woman.

Our stormy relationship turned into one of love-hate. When he would put me through the anxiety of not knowing where he was for days at a time, I hated him. But when he came back and we made up, I loved him.

Frank's strength and protectiveness were a strong attraction for me. My dad had those same traits. He would do anything to protect his kids, even if he didn't agree with what we were doing.

Once, Frank had been charged with assault to commit murder and the police were looking for him. They went to my dad's house in the middle of the night.

My dad jumped out of bed and headed down the hallway. The pounding and incessant ringing of the doorbell made him furious. It would scare everyone in the house half to death.

The house was surrounded with county officers, metro officers and a Special Enforcement Squad. They had enough guns and ammunition to start a war.

"What do you want?" my dad snapped.

"We want Frank Costantino," the officer said.

"You come pounding on my door at 2 a.m. looking for Frank? You haven't got the guts to come during the day? I don't believe it! You're looking for one man, and you bring 50 people with you. You know very well that he's not here. You scared my family half to death! You guys are crazy and I ain't telling you nothin!"

They backed off and my dad slammed the door. He wouldn't have surrendered Frank even if he were in the house.

I admired that kind of loyalty and backbone. But sometimes Frank's strength and protectiveness had negative effects on me. His strength could turn into control and his protectiveness into a jealous rage. Like the incident with the motorcycle gang . . .

In 1967 we were living in a modern apartment complex. There were two Spanish-style white stucco buildings that faced each other with a pool and courtyard between them. A wrought-iron balcony ran the length of the buildings on the second-story level. A decorative brick divider with built-in mailboxes gave privacy to the pool area.

We were renting a two-bedroom apartment on the first floor and our friends, Dottie and Rene, were in a second-floor apartment in the building across from us.

A group of us were going to a party that night and my friend Rusty stopped by to see if we were ready. Frank was still getting dressed and told us to go on ahead and wait for him over at Dottie and Rene's.

Loud music blared from one of the apartments above us. Members of a local motorcycle gang, wearing leather jackets, had come roaring in on their bikes to join the party already in progress. The tiny apartment couldn't contain all the people and many of them spilled out onto the balcony.

They shouted and swore above the din of the music. Everyone guzzled beer. I glanced up as Rusty and I stepped out into the courtyard and was glad that wasn't the party we were going to.

"Hey, baby, how about coming up here and partying with us?"

It was one of the gang members. He was short, stocky, with black curly hair and a beer belly which overflowed the chair he was sitting in.

"Just ignore him, Rusty," I said.

More voices joined in and the wolf whistles began.

"I got something for you, baby!"

"What you need is a real man!"

"Just keep walking, Rusty," I said as we hurried across the courtyard. "Hopefully, Frank won't hear them."

"Why worry about Frank?" Rusty asked.

"You just don't know Frank," I said. "He'd take it personally and blow them away."

We went up to Dottie's apartment, ignoring the whistles and smart remarks.

"What's going on out there?" Dottie asked.

The next thing we heard was, "You're going to wind up in that pool!" Someone just kept repeating it, slowly, with relish.

I opened the door and there was Frank backing this guy towards the pool, holding a gun at his head. Frank's friend, Artie, was following behind, taunting the guy.

"You're dead, man ... You're going to end up face down in the pool."

"My god, Bunny, he's going to kill him. Do something!" Rusty panicked.

I yelled, "Frank, let it go. It's not worth it!"

Dottie was terrified and ran for the phone. I heard her calling the cops, telling them there was a fight going on — — and someone was sure going to get killed.

"The cops are coming, Frank. Just let it go!"

The guy realized Frank was serious about blowing him away and said nervously, "Frank, hey man, come on, You're Italian, I'm Italian, we're gumbas."

"You ain't nothin!" Frank roared in his raspy Italian voice. "If you even breathe, I'm going to spread your brains all over this place!"

The piercing wail of police sirens rolled across the courtyard. Everybody bolted for the apartments. When the police arrived on the scene, nobody was around.

Frank was boiling and wanted to know who called the cops.

"I did," Dottie said. "I was terrified. I figured if you didn't kill him, he was going to kill you, or turn that whole motorcycle gang loose on this place. I was just trying to prevent a murder." She was trembling.

"Forget it," Frank said. "Let's go to the party."

"Party!" Rusty screamed. "Who wants to party now?

Frank walked out and Rusty said, "Why do you stay married to a madman like that? Doesn't he realize this isn't a game? We could all be dead!"

That was so typical of Frank. He could regain his control and walk away from a situation feeling "cool," but leave everyone else in shambles. Especially me.

Later that night, lying in bed, I thought back over what Rusty and Dottie had said. What kind of a man was I married to? Sometimes he was so hard, a mass of hair-triggered violence. It was as though he only felt really alive when he was fighting or challenging someone to fight.

I confronted him with my feelings and he said, "Look, Bunny, I love you and the kids, but this is the way I choose to live my life. I don't think you're treated so badly. You have a nice place to live, diamonds, money. What more do you want? There are a lot of women, including some of your friends, that would love to have what you have."

"Yeah, they think living with you is exciting, but do they realize the agony that comes along with it? They might want the glamour and glitter, but would they share the pain?" I shouted.

He mumbled something about my being ungrateful and rolled over and went to sleep. Just like that. Didn't care at all. While every nerve ending in my body was frazzled.

As I lay there brooding, I began to have heart palpitations. It felt as though my heart had tripled in speed. My hands were sweaty and I was having difficulty in breathing. My whole body was trembling, but I managed to crawl out of bed and to the phone. I wanted my father.

By the time he arrived my whole body had broken into a cold sweat and I could hardly stand up. We woke Frank up, and he stayed home with the kids while my dad drove me to the hospital.

When the doctor examined me, my heartbeat was up to 200 and my blood pressure was dropping. He gave me a shot of digitalis, started an I.V., and ordered an electrocardiogram. I thought I was going to die.

I spent 24 hours in the intensive care unit before my heart rate began slowing to normal.

Frank came in, but I was so exhausted I didn't care if he was there or not. He slipped a huge diamond on my finger and mumbled something about looking up the motorcycle gang and getting even for this.

Laying in a hospital bed gave me time to reflect on our marriage. Things were out of kilter. The excitement had gone too far. I felt a desperate need to get life under control. Frank was in too deep and I was scared. It was okay at first, but now everything was moving too fast for me.

When I finally came home, I tried reasoning with him to go legitimate. "This is too much for me, Frank. It's not a game anymore. We've got to stop."

"Well, I don't see it that way," he said. "This is what you bought into and it's the way it's going to be."

"If things don't change, I don't see how we can make it together and I want you to leave," I said.

"This is my place and I'm not leaving," he yelled.

"Fine. Then I'll leave," I screamed.

We didn't speak to each other for the next few days and he stayed away most of the time. I knew he was seeing another woman.

Some friends of mine let me use their apartment for a few weeks while they went up north on a vacation. I began looking for a place of my own to rent.

Whenever I saw a vacancy sign in front of an apartment building I would go in and inquire, but as soon as they heard my name was Bunny Costantino, the vacancy would suddenly be filled. I was furious.

I confronted Frank with what was happening. "What have you done? I can't get an apartment anywhere!"

"I ain't done nothin," he said.

"Well, if I don't find a place in the next few days, my friends will be back and I'll be out on the street."

"You really want out?" he asked.

"Yes."

"Fine," he said indifferently. "Just go back to the apartments on 29th street. I'll make a phone call and you'll have a place by tomorrow."

The next day I went to the 29th street apartments and sure enough, there were now several vacancies to choose from.

This was our first separation while Frank was out on the street and it felt strange. My suspicions about him seeing another woman were confirmed. He had a girlfriend in a small town about 30 miles north of Miami.

I began to date occasionally, too, and that infuriated Frank. His anger didn't make sense to me. I didn't understand him. I had come to a place where my marriage didn't seem salvageable.

Chapter 3

After Frank and I were split up for awhile, I went back to him. I was still tense and worried about him while we were separated and decided I was better off with him than without him. I might as well enjoy the luxuries and the high life while I could.

He was making the headlines in the newspapers because of his arrests in connection with some major robberies.

He always hired a good lawyer and beat the rap, but inside me was that vague foreboding that he wouldn't be able to beat them all. So my attitude became one of "eat, drink, and be merry . . . "

The day Frank came home with a new Buick Wildcat that he had just paid cash for, I said to him, "You know, Frank, that car would sure look good parked in the driveway of a new house."

I knew he didn't want to be bothered with the responsibility of a house and he just gave me one of his "forget it" looks. He preferred luxury apartment living.

"If you can buy a new car, why can't you buy me a new house?" I said. "We certainly can afford it."

"I thought 'things' weren't important to you," he said. "What happened to all your speeches about me dropping out of this business?"

"You'll never change, " I snapped, "so why shouldn't I live in luxury while I can?"

"Fine," he laughed, "You want a house? We'll buy a house."

The realtor who took us through some model lakefront homes asked Frank what he did for a living.

"I'm a burglar," Frank said, smiling.

The realtor glanced at him and then laughed. "All kidding aside, " he asked, "What do you really do for a living?"

Frank looked straight in his eyes and said, "I told you, I'm a burglar."

The realtor cleared his throat and smiled nervously. He kept fidgeting with his papers as he showed us the rest of the homes.

When we got outside I said to Frank, "Are you crazy? You'll blow our chance of buying one of these houses!"

"Don't worry about it. As long as we've got a big cash down payment, they'll give us the loan. They don't care where the money comes from, as long as they get their share."

He was right. They approved our loan and we bought a house.

I loved being back in a home of my own. I was tired of apartment living. It was a large three-bedroom ranch, white stucco, with attractive stone work. A pleasant patio ran the whole length of the house in the back, overlooking the lake. The lawn gradually sloped down to the water, where we had our own private boat dock.

The landscaping was beautiful, with banana trees in the front yard along the circular drive. The antique garden plow I placed on the front lawn was the finishing touch.

An interior decorator helped me to plan the color scheme and choose the paint and wallpaper. I wanted new furniture to fit in with the decor so we spent $15,000 furnishing the house. I liked being able to go into a store and purchase anything I wanted without having to check the price tag.

I remember the bedroom set I picked out. It was Italian Provincial, with a king-size electric bed that went up and down in six positions on each side. I was showing it to one of my friends one day and she commented, "I sure wish we could afford something like that."

"It's yours," I said.

She looked at me in disbelief. I shrugged my shoulders and said, "No big deal. Frank can afford another one."

We went through quite a few items that way. When I tired of something I would just give it away and get another one. Frank would get upset at times and say that he bought something as a token of his love and be angry that I gave it away. But I didn't see it that way. Money was easy. Why not spread a little around?

Then there were the minks and the jewelry. Once Frank came home with an eight carat diamond for me worth $30,000. I also had one with 20 diamonds on it, shaped like a beehive. That's the one I lost under the clothesline in the back yard. Never did find it.

Frank gambled away a lot of money at the crap tables, but there seemed to be an endless supply. Once when a friend of mine was over, we walked in on my son Tony, age two, tearing up $100 bills. He had discovered the $20,000 Frank had stashed in the coffee table drawer and was playing with it. I was mortified, but Frank roared. He thought it was hilarious. My friend never dared question me about it.

My large wardrobe was another thing I was proud of. I had something for every occasion. The only problem was deciding what to wear. Like the night we were going to The Deauville to see Sammy Davis, Jr. perform.

I tried on one dress after another and just tossed them on the bed. Then I put on the see-through crocheted dress and stood in front of the full-length mirror. I still had a good figure, even after having several babies. I had been to the hairdresser and my dark hair was teased into a beehive hairdo. I sighed and decided the dress was a bit provocative considering the fact that The Deauville was such an elegant place. I took it off and tossed it on top of the others on the bed.

There was a vague discontent within me – unformed, unshaped, but there nonetheless. I should be happy. I had everything a woman could want. What's wrong?

I brushed aside the thoughts and chose a black clingy cocktail dress, silver spike-heeled sandals, diamond necklace and earrings, and my new white silver mink.

Brian and Delores were already there when we arrived. Brian was a good friend of Frank's and they had pulled off some armed robberies together. He was Spanish, tall and slender with brown wavy hair. I straightened his hair for him once when he and Frank were going on a stick-up. He wanted to be identified as a businessman with straight hair.

Brian was divorced and dating Delores. She came slinking toward us in her skin-tight, red-sequined dress. As she whirled around in front of us, she said, "Isn't this dress exquisite? I got it on sale for only $150. Wasn't that a fantastic bargain?"

I managed a smile.

"Oh, Bunny, your hair looked so much better the way you used to wear it," she continued. "This is not you at all."

My smile was fading when the maitre d' came over to usher us to our table. Frank and I went first, and I very dramatically slipped off my silver mink, dragging it behind me on the floor. I could play the game too.

When we were seated at our table, I noticed someone sitting nearby who looked familiar. I asked Frank if he knew who it was.

"Flip Wilson," he said. Then I remembered having seen him on television. I looked around at the people. The men were dressed in fancy suits or tuxedos, the women in their diamonds and furs. So this is what it means to "arrive."

I managed small talk with Delores over dinner, but I didn't like her and she didn't like me. It was a cold war. I just couldn't understand why Brian stuck it out with her. She wasn't his type, and I felt he could do better.

Delores had quite a reputation of her own, with many of her escapades attracting the news media. She made a lot of money and lived in high style.

Brian moved into her elegant home on the bay front, with the heart-shaped swimming pool, rolling lawns, Cadillac convertible – all the "good things" of life. But they paid the ultimate price.

We heard about it on the news. It was reported as a gangland execution. Apparently she had double-crossed someone in a deal. The only reason Brian was killed was because he happened to be with her and could identify them. He was just in the wrong place at the wrong time.

They said Brian was knocked out before he was shot and probably never knew what hit him. He was tied up and gagged, and three bullets were pumped into his head. But Delores had been beaten beyond recognition before being shot.

The police came knocking on our door that night. Frank was considered a prime suspect because of a fight he had had with Brian a week earlier over some money Brian owed Frank.

They asked Frank if he did it and wanted to know where he was at the time of the murder.

"No, man, I didn't do it. Brian was my friend." Frank gave them his alibi and they said they would check it out.

"Well, that narrows it down to about 400 suspects," they said. "She lived hard and fast, a real high roller, but she sure paid a hell of a price for it."

The stark reality of the kind of life we were into crept over me. What if somebody got really mad at Frank and came to kill him and I was here? They'd kill me. They'd kill the kids, too.

Later that night as we lay in bed, neither one of us could sleep. Frank didn't say anything, but he was tossing and turning. There was nothing inside me but a cold, grey fear.

After Brian's death, everything went sour. I began having anxiety attacks. Everything seemed unsettled and unsettling. I felt as if I were on an emotional roller coaster and out of control of my life.

The instability of our whole situation was brought home to me when I got the news that Johnny Wop had committed suicide. He was the last guy I thought would do something like that.

I had to be the one to break it to my friend Pat. She and Johnny had split up, but she still cared for him and I knew it would hit her hard.

My whole body was trembling as I tried to choke out the words. I blinked rapidly, trying to hold back the tears.

"He got arrested in Tampa, selling drugs to a narc,

and was convinced he was going to prison. He was terrified and went into a deep depression."

My voice broke and I felt the hot tears rising behind my eyes. Pat sat there, rigid, her whole body tense, while I was talking to her. She sensed what I was about to say.

"He decided to end it all . . . and took an overdose of heroin," I said. "Johnny's dead."

Pat started trembling and her whole body shook with sobs. I walked over to her and held her.

As we wept in each other's arms, the policeman's words surfaced in my mind . . .

"Sure is a hell of a price to pay . . . "

Chapter 4

I was born on March 2, 1945, in Whitinsville, a small town in Central Massachusetts. I enjoyed growing up in New England . . . searching the woods for pussy willows in the spring, picking blueberries in the summer, swimming at Kiwanis Beach on hot summer days, jumping in piles of crisp fall leaves, building snowmen in the fresh wet snow with the cold winter wind stinging my cheeks.

My father, William Avedisian, was an avid fisherman and would be out fishing as soon as the season opened. He had a fourteen-foot Fiberglas boat with a 25-horsepower motor.

He and I spent many quiet days together on the water. We would pack a lunch that included sandwiches, a six-pack of beer for him and Pepsi for me.

In the early dawn we would anchor the boat out on Wallum Lake in Douglas. From all directions came the soft sounds and sights of wildlife awakening – an awkward turtle started from his perch on a rock; a squirrel scampering along the shoreline; a flock of ducks flying overhead.

My father would put a worm on each of our hooks and we would sit quietly, basking in the warm sunshine, watching our bobbers dance on the shimmering water. The gentle lap of waves on the side of the boat would make me feel sleepy. I didn't care if we ever caught any fish. I just enjoyed being with my dad.

My father was my idea of what a man should be. He had broad shoulders and a thick barrel chest. His hair was thick and black and curled slightly around his temples. He had a firm, hard handshake and when he talked to you, he looked you straight in the eye. He worked hard and loved his family and I thought he was at least ten feet tall. I always felt I was somehow special to him and I loved him dearly.

I never felt that way about Mary, my mother. It seemed no matter what I did or how hard I tried, I was second-rate in her eyes. She was attractive with an olive complexion and rich, shiny black hair. She dieted often and kept her figure slim and in shape.

Perhaps it was her hardness that set her apart from me. Perhaps it was the way she whined and complained. She had been spoiled when she was younger, and now, as I was growing up, I sensed a feeling of distance, a gulf that separated us. She placed much of the responsibility for us onto my dad. Her idea of discipline was to scream, "Wait until your father gets home."

There were four children in our family: Carol, the oldest by seven years, was blind. Paula, my other sister, was a year younger than me. The youngest was Billy, who was four years younger than me.

Sunday was family day. My dad would get up before the rest of us and cook a big breakfast, his own version of "eggs on the island." We'd each get an egg and several slices of bacon with hot V-8 juice poured over the top.

This became a tradition and even after we were all married my dad expected us to be there for Sunday breakfast. He felt secure with all of us under his wing. He would have liked us all living next door to him so he could watch over us, no matter how old we were.

After breakfast we would go to church and then on to the beach for a picnic, a lazy drive to buy ice cream cones, or a trip down to Youngsma's Field where my dad kept his Steerman double winger and later his Piper Cub. He would give everyone rides, including the kids who hung around at the field. I was afraid of flying, so when my turn came up he would just taxi around the runway. I felt so proud peering out the tiny window and waving at everyone.

Dad was a tool and dye maker and designed a number of inventions for the machines he worked on . He received a bonus for these and decided to buy a new car with the extra money. I was about six years old at the time and he took me along to the dealer's showroom.

"Which car do you like, Bunny?" he asked.

I pointed at the shiny red convertible. He laughed and said, "That's not very practical for a family car."

He walked away to check out the other cars and I started crying. "I want this one!"

He came back, chuckling at my persistence, and said, "Okay, okay. We'll take it out for a ride." I saw him wink at the dealer and wasn't sure what that meant.

We drove through town with the top down and I sat like a princess in the front seat. He tooted the horn as we pulled into our driveway, and my mother came outside.

"You've got to be kidding, Bill," she said when she saw the car. "You can't be serious about keeping this."

"Well, to tell you the truth, I was just going to take it for a ride, but now I really like it," he said. "Why don't you hop in and I'll take you for a spin around the block?"

"I don't want any part of it," she snapped as she stormed back toward the house.

My dad heaved a big sigh as he opened his door. I scrambled across the front seat and got out on his side.

"Convertibles are not safe for children," she started in again. "They make me nervous!"

"I make the decisions around here, and we're keeping it!" he shouted.

He stood his ground for about three months. Then he traded it in for a station wagon.

My sister, Carol, was a boarding student at Perkins School for the Blind in Watertown, Massachusetts. We would pick her up for the weekend on Saturday mornings. The school had a beautiful campus and my dad would let Paula, Billy and me romp around on the rolling lawns while waiting for Carol to finish her piano and voice lessons. We thought it was neat having a sister that lived away from home.

Carol would often babysit for us when my parents went out. We would try to get away with things because she was blind, but she seemed to have a built-in radar and always knew where we were and what we were doing. She could swing a mean dust mop when she had to!

She was popular and did a lot of dating. She especially loved to dance. When she was at school during the week Paula and I would try on all her dresses and gowns and pretend we were out dancing too.

We enjoyed having her home on weekends and she came to church with us on Sunday mornings.

I remember the Sunday my dad broke this tradition and refused to go to church. We had always been actively involved in Sunday school, choir and other church programs. The pastor and his wife often came to our house for dinner and my dad was a good donor to the church.

That all changed the day the letter arrived. The pastor had checked on my dad's salary at work. The letter stated that although his present donations were appreciated, my dad really ought to be giving more. He owed it to the church, the pastor said.

Dad stormed out the door with the letter clutched in his hand and drove right over to the parsonage.

"How dare you go and check on my income," he shouted. "You have no right to send me a letter like this, demanding that I increase my donations. It'll be a cold day in hell before you get another cent out of me!" He flung the letter in the pastor's face and stalked out.

He never went back to church, but my mother continued to take us kids for awhile. Gradually, she stopped attending also, except for Easter and Christmas.

Sometimes he would watch the religious programs on television on Sunday mornings. I remember him saying to my mother one time, "Mary, what do you think of this healing business this preacher is always talking about? Do you think it's real?"

She just looked at him and shrugged her shoulders.

In 1953 a fire destroyed our house and we stayed with relatives until we could relocate. My dad had often toyed with the idea of looking for a job in Southern California and settling there. Now that our house was gone, it seemed like the right time to do it.

Traveling with my dad was fun. He would stop at all the places of interest along the way, allowing us to fully absorb the scenery and historical sites. I remember the dusty old cowboy towns, the rickety covered wagons, and the herds of powerful buffalo. I pretended I was the wife of a gunfighter, riding in a stagecoach, as we traveled down the highway.

The road shimmered in the heat. A trailer crested

the hill in front of us and when I heard the hiss of its powerful air brakes, I pretended it was a train being stopped and robbed by my husband, the famous gunfighter. It was all very exciting to my imaginative eight-year-old mind.

The Grand Canyon was awesome and the Painted Desert in Arizona was beautiful at sunset, the rolling mountains splashed with brilliant pastel colors.

My dad made sure there was a swimming pool at each motel. We had fun splashing each other and unwinding from a long day in the car. My mother just watched us, sitting in a lounge chair on the side of the pool. She wasn't enthusiastic about the move because she would be so far away from her mother. She sulked most of the trip.

One of the stops my father insisted on making was in St. Louis. He heard that a faith healer was having tent meetings there and wanted to take Carol. None of the doctors had been able to restore her sight; maybe this man could help. When we arrived, my dad asked who was in charge of the meetings and went to talk with the elders.

They said the preacher would be happy to pray for Carol, and then added that a donation of $100 would be helpful to their organization. Dad hesitated, but then decided if Carol's eyesight was restored, it would be well worth it. So he wrote out a check and came back to the motel to get ready for the meeting.

Paula and I went along with Carol and my dad, but Billy stayed at the motel with my mother. On the way to the meeting Carol asked, "Daddy, do we have to go? I'll be so embarrassed."

"Wouldn't it be worth a little feeling of embarrassment if you walked out of that tent tonight with your eyesight?" he asked. "This guy claims to do miracles and it's not costing us anything, except a little self-consciousness." Then he checked himself and said, "Well, hardly anything."

The pungent smell of sawdust filled the huge tent. It reminded me of going to the circus. We slipped into the back row and sat on the hard wooden planks used for benches. Some people brought pillows or blankets to sit on. Within a short time the tent was filled to capacity. There were almost as many blacks as whites.

A happy-looking man stepped up to the podium and began leading the audience in singing. Soon everyone was clapping their hands and swaying to the rhythm of the music. This sure didn't seem like "church" to me.

Next, someone preached a seemingly endless sermon which I couldn't understand. The bench felt like concrete under me and I kept shifting from one side to the other. Carol was fidgeting with her handkerchief and Paula fell asleep with her head on my father's lap.

Some people seemed to be listening intently to what was being said and shouted "Amen!" from time to time. Others were just waiting to be prayed for, hoping to be healed.

People started to get out of their seats and walk down the aisles toward the front. "Daddy, where are they going?" I asked.

"They're getting in line to be prayed for," he said. "You and Paula stay here and wait while I take Carol up front."

"Do I have to go?" Carol whined.

"Come on, it'll be all right," my dad said.

I stared at them walking down the aisle, but then lost sight of them in the crowd. The procession reminded me of an assembly line in a factory. As each person got to the preacher, he would tap them firmly on the head and say, "You're healed" "You're healed." It was like a machine putting caps on bottles.

Finally, I spotted Carol and my dad coming back towards our seat. Carol was crying and my dad grumbled, "Come on, let's get out of here." I knew she wasn't healed. We drove back to the motel in silence.

The next day my mother and father hardly spoke to each other and when they did, they ended up in a fight. They argued over when to stop to eat, where to eat, and what to eat. I was glad when we reached our motel that night.

When we arrived in Long Beach, California, we stayed with some cousins while my dad went job hunting. I had headaches almost every day and my eyes were puffy and watery from the smog. Carol cried because she missed her friends back in Massachusetts. My mother complained about the cost of long distance phone calls to her mother. So after about a month, we left.

We traveled south through New Mexico and then over to Florida to visit relatives there, before heading back up to Massachusetts.

A short time later, my dad had a heart attack and we decided the warm climate in Florida would be better for his health. Once again we packed up and moved, this time to Hialeah, Florida, just north of Miami.

My sister Carol got married a year later and moved back to Massachusetts with her husband. She was seventeen. Paula, Billy and I soon made new friends and settled into the routine of school.

I enjoyed the Florida sunshine, the swaying palm trees, picking oranges, and swimming at the sandy ocean beaches. It was a happy time.

Chapter 5

I was a sixteen-year-old junior at Hialeah High School in the fall of 1961. Other than the social life, school held little interest to me. I wanted to attend vocational school and become a hairdresser, or take up nursing, but my mother ignored my pleas and insisted I take the Business Course at Hialeah High. It was more respectable, she said.

I knew she had left school herself at 16 and she had always wanted to be a secretary. Now she wanted to fulfill her dream through me. When I told her how much I hated the courses and wanted to switch, she just told me that I didn't know what I wanted.

At first I studied hard and got good grades, but when I saw that it didn't impress my mother, I just let them slide. It wasn't worth the effort.

She always made a big deal out of Billy's grades, though. And she let him switch to another school to study music. He was always the center of her attention; Paula and I were in the background.

She did want us to look good, however, and bought us nice clothes. My mother could sew and my dad wanted her to make some of our school clothes to cut down on expenses. Instead, she opened up a charge account behind his back because she didn't feel like sewing. When the bills came in they had a big fight, but he ended up paying them.

I remember the day my mother took a pile of my clothes out to the back yard and burned them because I hadn't done my ironing. She expected to get a big reaction from me, so I just ignored her. I knew she would just have to go out and buy me new ones, which she did.

On Tuesdays I had study hall last period so I would just skip and go over to The Stall, a small restaurant where everybody hung out. It was named in connection with the Hialeah Race Track. Saddles, bridles, jockey whips, and racing posters decorated the walls, creating the country-western atmosphere. "Stallions" and "Mares" were written over the restroom doors. I looked around to see if my boyfriend, Johnny, was here yet, but he wasn't. He must have decided to stay for his last period class.

"Hey, Bunny, over here." Several of my girlfriends were motioning for me to come sit at their table. They were talking with someone I hadn't seen around before.

"This is Frank Costantino."

"Nice to meet you, Bunny," he said as he stood and reached for my hand.

His hands were large and strong. He had dark curly hair, heavy eyebrows, and penetrating brown eyes. He flashed a smile and I felt my face flush as his dark eyes seemed to look right through me.

He had broad shoulders, narrow hips and muscular-looking biceps. There was a tattoo etched on each forearm. He wore a fresh white T-shirt tucked into a skin-tight pair of black dress pants.

"Frank was the Captain of the football team at Hialeah High a few years ago," Pat said. "Now he's into wrestling. He's billed as 'Frankie Carbo' in the newspaper article about Saturday night's match."

A horn tooted outside. "Here's our ride," Pat said.

"We've got to go. Hope to see you again sometime, Frank. Bye, Bunny."

"Does she always talk non-stop like that?" Frank asked.

I laughed and shrugged my shoulders.

"Where do you work?" he asked.

"I'm still in school," I said. "But I'd like to get a part time job somewhere."

"With your looks, you should be able to get a job anywhere. Just wear a short skirt and a tight sweater when you apply," he grinned. "They're always looking for girls at the motels on Miami Beach."

"That's not exactly what I had in mind," I said as I felt my face redden.

"Suit yourself," he said, as he got up to leave.

Just then Johnny walked in and said, "Hey Frank, how are you?

I didn't realize they knew each other. They didn't seem to have much in common. Johnny wasn't the playboy Frank appeared to be. He was short and slender with a boyish build. We had fun together, but our relationship wasn't anything heavy.

Frank gave Johnny a couple of free passes to the wrestling match for Saturday night and I agreed to go.

I had never been to a wrestling match before and found the atmosphere very exciting. Frank came over and talked to us for a few minutes before it was his turn in the ring. As he turned to leave, I jumped out of my seat and planted a kiss on his cheek.

"That's for good luck," I said.

Johnny was fuming when I sat down and didn't speak to me the rest of the night. Frank won the match and came with us to the Pizza Palace afterwards. Johnny was still mad and we ended up in an argument. I told him I wasn't going home with him and he took off out of the parking lot, tires screeching.

I spotted my sister Paula with some friends and walked over to their car. When I introduced Frank, Paula said, "Hey, are you old enough to buy us some beer?"

"If that's what you want, I can get it," Frank said.

We all piled into the car, Frank picked up a couple of six-packs, and we drove out to Miami Lakes.

Frank and I got out and went for a walk while the rest of the kids sat in the car drinking. There were several new houses being built in the area and we roamed through them.

"Some day I'll have a big house on a lake," he said as he took my hand.

He had an air of confidence about him that made me feel secure.

A few weeks later he called and asked me out. I was afraid my father would think he was too old for me. He was 21; I was 16. I accepted the date, but told Frank to act as young as he could with my dad when he came to pick me up.

Much to my surprise, my dad really liked him. In fact, they sat and talked and laughed together, and I thought we'd never get out of the house. It wasn't too long after that, however, that my dad changed his mind.

My mother had mentioned in a conversation that the grocery store she worked in had been robbed several times, but the burglar never found the safe.

"Why is that, Mary?" Frank asked.

"Because it's hidden in a place no one would think of looking," she chuckled. "It's in the base of the gumball machine."

Frank just grinned and made no further comment.

The next night the store was robbed again and this time the burglar found the safe. My mother suspected

Frank, but didn't dare confront him. My father insisted I stop dating him after that. But I continued to see him in secret.

I was bored with school and decided to quit and go to work at the Dairy Queen. My dad tried to convince me that I would be sorry for quitting later on, but I felt he just didn't understand.

Dad would pick me up after work at 11 p.m. and we would often stop by Mae and Dave's Restaurant and sit outside and talk. He would have beer and pizza, while I had a Coke and hot dog. I kept bringing up the subject of dating Frank, but he wouldn't give in.

"You don't want to go out with this guy, Bunny. He's already been arrested several times and your life with him would be miserable. He's going to spend his life in and out of jail. What kind of a life is that?"

"But dad, I've known other kids who did things like that. When they got married, they settled down."

"You're not going out with him and that's that," he said.

Every Friday night my dad would drive my sister Paula and me down to the highschool dance at 7 p.m. and pick us up again at 11 p.m. when it was over. I would walk inside, wait for my dad to leave, and then go out with Frank.

I felt that I was in love with him and told him one night that I was going to be the one to marry him.

"Sure you are," he laughed. Then he changed his tone and told me he loved me, but wasn't ready for marriage.

I knew that he occasionally dated others, like Dallas and Susie from the nightclub. They had their own apartment and Frank spent a lot of time there. He also was engaged to a girl named Maria back in Boston where his mother lived, but somehow I still felt we could make it together. I liked being known as 'Frank's girl', and we continued dating secretly for about a year.

He often bought me gifts and also gave me his highschool football trophies. I knew I was special to him because of this. We began to spend more and more time together.

I remember one day in particular when we were at the beach. It was a typical hot Miami summer day. The temperature was 100 degrees.

There was a small boy sitting alone on a nearby blanket, crying. Frank walked over to him and gently asked what was wrong.

"I'm hot and thirsty," he cried.

"Where are your parents?" Frank asked.

The boy pointed towards the lounge opposite the parking lot and said between sobs, "They went in there to get a beer and said they would be right back. But now I don't know where they are."

Frank said, "Come with me to the snack bar and I'll get you something cold to drink."

He took a towel, wiped the boy's face, and took him by the hand to the snack bar. When they came back, Frank sat on the blanket talking to him until his parents showed up a few hours later.

I realized then that Frank had a gentle side to him that I hadn't seen before. In fact, very few people saw this side of Frank. I wished my dad could see this part of Frank. Then maybe I wouldn't have to date him in secret.

Once Frank and I discussed the possibility of eloping, but when I thought it through, I decided I didn't want to hurt my dad that way. So we just continued to date without my parents' knowledge. I figured I was going to be 18 soon and then my dad would let me make my own decision.

A short time later Frank told me he was flying to Boston to see his mother. But I knew Maria lived there too, and I asked him if he planned to see her while there.

He admitted that he did. He hadn't seen Maria in over a year and hardly ever talked about her, so I had assumed everything was over between them.

What if he sees her and his feelings for me change? What if he decides to stay there? The questions made me feel very insecure. I loved him so much. How could I live without him? My whole world would cave in around me.

The following week I discovered I was pregnant.

For about a month I tried calling Frank in Boston, but he was never in when I called and even though I left messages, he never returned my calls. I was beginning to feel desperate and was afraid my parents would find out I was pregnant before I had a chance to talk to Frank.

When I finally reached him, he said he'd been in jail and didn't know about my calls.

"Well, I called to tell you I'm pregnant," I said.

"Oh god," he sighed.

"What are you going to do about it?" I demanded. "Are you going to marry me?"

After a long pause he said, "Why don't you just go ahead and use my name as the father and I'll pay for any expenses?"

"In other words, you're not going to marry me."

"Bunny, that's the last thing I need right now."

"I can't believe you don't care about me any-more," I said.

The whole conversation was stiff and awkward for both of us. After I hung up, I burst into tears and couldn't stop crying. How could he not love me anymore? Was there still something between him and Maria? Then my mother came into the room and everything came spilling out of me.

"Oh, my god, your father's going to kill me," she said. "I knew you were still dating Frank and I never told him."

After she regained her composure, she said, "Well, you have only two choices. Either you get him to marry you, or you have an abortion."

I stared at her in disbelief and suddenly felt very ill.

"You'll have to tell your father," she stated.

"Why can't you tell him?" I pleaded.

She just ignored me and continued, "Tonight I'm going out for a while and when I return, you'd better have told him."

I was angry and hurt. All she could think about was herself. What about me? I was the one who was pregnant. Didn't my feelings count for anything?

Later that night my dad and I were sitting on the front porch.

"Dad?"

"Hmmm?"

"Oh, never mind," I said.

We sat there in silence for a while and then I asked, "Dad, was there ever something you wanted to tell your parents, but you were afraid to because of what their reaction might be?"

He turned and looked at me and I knew I had his full attention. I blinked back the tears.

"I'm pregnant," I said.

He was quiet for a while and then asked, "Who's the father?"

"Frank Costantino."

He let out a long, heavy sigh as he buried his face in

his hands. "Couldn't you have picked someone else? Out of all my daughters, you're the one I most looked forward to walking down the aisle. You're such a pretty girl. I don't understand why you had to pick someone like Frank." He was hurt. "You'll have no life with him at all," he said as he slowly got up and walked into the house.

I felt heartbroken that I had caused him pain and had let him down. I needed his support and wondered how this would affect our relationship.

My parents went round and round the next few days, arguing about what to do. I felt a distance between my dad and me. It was obvious he was disappointed in me.

My mother pushed him into checking about an abortion, but he was told it was dangerous and wouldn't go along with it.

"She should just keep the baby," he said.

"But, Bill, if she doesn't get married, what will we tell our friends?" she said.

"Our friends will understand. The others don't matter," he said.

"You know," she said slowly, "with Frank's record, I bet he wouldn't want to have to face charges for unlawful intercourse and contributing to the delinquency of a minor."

"Mom!" I screamed, "You wouldn't!"

She gave me the kind of look that told me I had nothing to say in the matter.

The next day she dragged me down to the State Attorney's Office. It was one of the worst days of my life. The questions were so humiliating.

Had I ever gone to bed with anyone else? Had Frank seduced me, or had I seduced him? Did I know that he could get five to ten years for this? You know, you'll have to answer some pretty embarrassing questions in court.

We drove home in silence and I felt really sick. My head throbbed. How could my mother put me through all this abuse? I hated her for it. It was obvious she cared about no one but herself.

When we got home, she got right on the phone and tried reaching Frank in Boston. He wasn't in, so she spoke to his mother and told her we were filing charges against Frank, unless he agreed to marry me. I went into the bathroom and took one of my mother's tranquilizers.

When Frank's mother told him what was going on, he said it wasn't right for me to have to take the heat alone, so he would come down and face it with me. But he was making no promises about marriage.

When he came back, all the emotions I had for him were stirred up and I felt so awkward. Without my knowledge, my mother told him that if he would marry me, I would divorce him after I had the baby and he would be free again.

When he came and told me he would marry me, he didn't mention what my mother had said. He assumed that I knew about it, but, of course, I did not.

"I'll try to make it up to you by being a good wife," I said.

A few days later we headed for the judges' chambers to be married by the justice of the peace. Frank bought me a black maternity outfit to wear and my sister and friend showed up in black too. The color blended well with the atmosphere.

Frank stood with his fists clenched and stumbled over the words as he repeated them after the justice of the peace. I was so relieved when it was over.

The next day we flew up to Boston and moved into a small apartment above Frank's mother. Any renewed hope I had for a working relationship between Frank and me was soon crushed.

He went out a lot and left me alone. One night he ordered me to iron a shirt for him.

"I'm going out," he said.

"Where are you going?" I asked.

"I'm going out with Maria," he said.

I just stared at him.

"Look, the only promise I made was to marry you long enough to give the baby a name. He slammed the door as he went out.

I went to the nearest phone booth and called my dad. "Daddy, please let me come home," I cried, "I can't take this anymore."

"Bunny, try to stick it out a while longer. He might change his mind when he sees the baby. If he doesn't, I'll send you the plane fare and you can come home then."

Maria was constantly harping at Frank about me and a strain developed in their relationship. After my daughter Lori Ann was born, Frank came into my hospital room all excited. He just loved the baby and was so proud to be a father.

"I want you to know that I'm breaking off with Maria," he said, "and I'm going to try to make a go of things with you."

I felt a sudden rush of hope. We would be a family, just the three of us.

But our fresh start was short-lived. The day I got out of the hospital Frank got arrested and put in jail in Dedham. When his case came up, he was given a one year sentence and had to serve six months in Billerica House of Corrections.

I was homesick and decided to fly back to Florida with Lori and stay with my parents until Frank got out. He came down six months later and got a job.

My dad loaned us money so we could settle into our own place. Frank worked long hours, but was only making minimum wage and the bills continued to pile up.

Then I got pregnant with our second child and with the extra expense of the doctor bills, finances were even tighter. Frank decided it wasn't worth working such long hours for only a small amount of money and before long he went back to stealing.

At first I was upset, but at least we could pay the bills. As long as the money was there, I decided I didn't care where it came from anymore.

The only thing I felt bad about was that my dad and family had to be affected by our life-style. Dad stood by us, but I knew it bothered him. I remember in particular the time Frank was on the run from the cops and I was with him, along with our two kids, Lori and Tony.

Frank was in a lot of trouble in Miami. In addition to the cops, there were underworld conflicts. I phoned my father and told him there was some trouble and we were going to Massachusetts for a while.

My sister Paula was married and she and her husband Harry were living in Whitinsville, Massachusetts. They had only been there for a short time and still had Florida license plates on their car.

The police knew we had relatives in Massachusetts and notified the authorities there to keep a watch out for us. Whitinsville is a small town and when the teletype came through at the police station about Frank, they immediately went to Paula and Harry's apartment to investigate.

They checked out the Florida plates and then talked to my Uncle Charlie who owned the apartments. They warned him not to let us in if we happened to show up. He could be charged with harboring a criminal.

After they left, my uncle went to Paula and Harry's. "Don't you dare let Frank and Bunny in if they show up, or you could end up in jail yourself," he warned.

Paula was so scared. How could she turn her own sister away? And yet, what if she let us in and then really did have to face charges? Or worse yet, the underworld?

Every time a car drove up the street that night, Paula and Harry sat up in bed. Is that Frank and Bunny? If they knock on the door, shall we let them in? It was a long night with little sleep.

In the morning, Paula called my father because she was so worried about me and the kids. He took the next flight to Boston.

We were staying someplace else in Massachusetts, but Frank said it would be okay if I went to visit Paula. I was completely surprised to find my father at the house when I arrived.

He was so relieved to see me. "I couldn't stand being down in Florida, not knowing what was going on with you and the kids." he said.

I assured him we were all right, but he wasn't convinced. He tried to get me to take the kids and fly back to Florida with him.

"I can't just abandon Frank like that," I said. "The heat will be off soon. Then we'll be back."

"You know you're the same way, Dad. You wouldn't cut and run either."

He was angry at Frank for what he was putting us through. I didn't tell him that Frank's mother had contacted us and said the F.B.I. had been there. They told her that Frank was suspected of killing 13 men.

The years of crime that followed were more than I had bargained for, however . . .The shootings, the tension, the violence, the deaths of Brian and Delores, Johnny Wop's suicide – the price tag was just too high.

I was so full of fear, I couldn't sleep at night. I began to lose weight. I was always on edge. My heart began to give me problems again and I was in and out of the hospital several times.

I was so relieved when Frank finally agreed to end his life of crime and go legitimate. But, without my knowledge, he planned what was going to be his last big robbery. He figured it would put us on Easy Street for the rest of our lives. Then he would go straight and put all his efforts into Decor Originals, a company he had purchased.

The Adrian Thal Fur Salon was one of the expensive shops along Coral Gables' Miracle Mile. There were $5,000,000 in furs stored in its vaults. Frank decided to hit it on Easter Sunday morning. It was all carefully planned. He had the blueprints of the stores, knew the patrol schedules, and had a buyer for the furs. He trusted the two guys that were with him.

But when they were cutting through the door of the vault, there was a single, unmapped alarm connected directly to the police station. Within minutes, the place was surrounded. Frank grabbed a phone and called me. "Bunny, what's the phone number of my bondsman? I'm at Adrian Thal's and the cops have surrounded the place. I'm about to be arrested."

I gave him the number and slammed the receiver down. Any dream I had for a new beginning was just an empty delusion now. I slumped into a chair and began to cry.

Chapter 6

A year after he was arrested for the Adrian Thal fur case, Frank was sentenced to 22½ years in prison, but managed to stay out on appeal bonds for the next two years. During that time he continued to steal. He also developed Decor Originals, a legitimate business manufacturing plaster-of-paris items for home decoration.

The police harrassed Frank constantly and were always picking him up, trying to tack some screwy charge on him. One night they pulled him over when he was driving my car. They searched the car without permission, and while they were searching it, one of the cops planted a pistol under the seat. Then they charged Frank with possession of firearms by a convicted felon. The Miami judge, Carling Stedman, ordered him to immediately begin serving time.

Frank's lawyer went to the State Supreme Court in Tallahassee to get the order changed and a Justice of the Supreme Court, Millard Caldwell, ordered Frank released on bond again. The chief of the sheriff's jail division was caught between conflicting orders and didn't know what to do with Frank. He finally obeyed the Miami judge's orders and at 4 a.m. the next morning shipped Frank off to Raiford.

That was in February, 1968. We were living in Miami. Raiford State Prison was 300 miles away. I received a letter from the Parole Board saying that Frank's expiration date was 1979.

"Oh, my god," I thought, "eleven years. What will I do? How can I wait that long? I would be 34 years old when he got out. What if I waited for him, and a month after he got out, he got arrested again?" I figured my whole life would be wasted just waiting for him.

I had always heard nasty rumors about Raiford. I knew Frank could handle himself on the street, but now he would be isolated from his friends, and could be outnumbered. There were at least two inmates in Raiford who wanted Frank dead. Would he even make it through the 11 years alive? This terrible question, and the others I was facing, made the next few days just a blur.

I felt weak and nauseous and finally went to the doctor. He told me I was pregnant again. He said my health was not good and suggested I consider having an abortion. Also, I had been taking Inderal for my heart problems and he said it wasn't known what effect the drug would have on the baby.

Driving home from the doctor's office, I felt the new fears compete in my mind with the ones already there.

Would the baby be deformed? What if I have one of my attacks during labor? When I had asked the doctor about this, he just shook his head and didn't answer me. If something happened to me, who would take care of the kids? My parents wouldn't be able to cope with them. Dad had just been told he had cancer. The doctors gave him less than a year to live.

And yet, an abortion seemed all wrong. What if my mother had her way with my first pregnancy and I had been forced into an abortion. I wouldn't have Lori. And I loved her so much.

I decided not to have the abortion, despite what the doctor had said.

I began to feel much better in the latter half of the pregnancy and in my eighth month I asked the doctor if he thought it would be all right for me to make the 600-mile round trip to Raiford to visit Frank. He saw no problem with it, as long as I didn't do the driving.

It would be good to see Frank again. The time dragged while he was gone. I knew he'd enjoy seeing the kids, too. Lori was five, Tony was three, and Rocco, one.

Visiting hours were from 9 a.m. to 3 p.m. on Sundays only. I decided to go by bus. I had to leave at 11 p.m. Saturday, travel through the night, and would arrive at 6:30 a.m. Sunday.

After we arrived at the bus station in Raiford, I bought some breakfast for the kids in a nearby restaurant. My stomach was in knots. I didn't eat. I felt like I had been on the bus for 20 hours.

From the restaurant I took a cab to the prison. It was 9 a.m., but there was already a long line of visitors formed outside the guardhouse.

It was a stifling hot day. The sun beat down unmercifully as we stood in line. I was glad I had Bermuda shorts on under my maternity top. Most of the women had slacks on. They must not have realized what a hot day it was going to be.

As I stood in line waiting, I wondered if Frank had changed. What would we talk about. Would he really be glad to see the kids, I wondered?

The kids got restless after a few hours in line and I was constantly yelling at Lori and Tony not to wander off. I was holding Rocco and he got heavier as the minutes ticked by. I was relieved when my turn came to step inside the gatehouse.

A guard pointed at a door with the sign "Women" on it and barked, "Through there."

When I stepped through the door, I was face to face with a stocky, grim-faced matron. Her brown hair was pulled back into a tight bun and her dark eyes flashed with hostility. She wore no makeup, had a sharp jaw and an equally sharp tongue.

"You first!" she snapped at Lori as she began frisking her.

"We need to be frisked?" I asked.

She totally ignored me and moved on to Tony.

Then she snatched Rocco out of my arms, laid him on a table, and removed his diapers. Frisking a baby! I didn't believe it.

Then she turned to me. I stepped back as she came towards me. She knew this was my first visit and was enjoying every minute of it. I stiffened as her rough, sweaty hands made their way in and out of every crevice on my body. I was flooded with a sense of humiliation and anger. She was treating me like a piece of garbage, the scum of the earth.

"You're not going to be able to go in," she barked like an army sergeant. "Shorts are not appropriate dress for visitors to wear."

I stood there rigid, my hands still clinched. I felt the hot tears rising behind my eyes, but I didn't let them reach my face.

"What am I supposed to wear?"

"Read the Visiting Regulations and check under 'Female Visitors, Appropriate Dress'," she said. She motioned me out.

I felt devastated as I walked back outside. If she knew I couldn't go in with shorts on , why did she bother to frisk me? Anger seethed within me as I realized how unnecessary that had been.

One of the inmate's wives who had been standing in line near me came over and asked what happened.

"I didn't realize they had a dress code," I said. "I don't know what I'm going to do."

She offered to give me a ride to a store so that I could buy something to wear. I thanked her for being willing to give up her place in line.

Because it was Sunday, most stores were closed. We finally found a little grocery store in town that sold a limited amount of clothing and other items. They didn't have any maternity clothes, so I just bought the largest dress on the rack. It was a bit snug through the stomach, and it went down to my ankles, but it would have to do.

It was raining when we stepped outside of the store. "We need rain, but why today?" I moaned. "My hair will be ruined."

"We've got to hustle," Mary said. "Visiting hours are only until 3 p.m. and it's close to noon already."

As she drove us back to the prison, I said, "It's a good thing I bought a round trip ticket for the bus. This dress cost me $5 and all I have left is some change."

I thanked Mary for helping me and went back over to the gatehouse at Union Correctional.

The matron smirked when she saw my dress. She checked the inmate list and informed me that Frank wasn't even on it.

"That's impossible," I said. "He's got to be on it."

"There are three prisons here at Raiford," she clipped. "Union Correctional, Florida State Prison, and the O Unit. Check at the State Prison. It's just down the road a ways."

I stepped out into the pouring rain with the kids and walked toward the guards' tower at the Maximum Security Unit of Florida State Prison. I picked up the phone outside the tower and the guard inside said, "State your business."

"I'm Mrs. Costantino and I'm here to visit my husband, Frank Costantino," I said.

I had to wait while he called inside to find out if Frank was there. My dress and the kids were clinging to me. I felt like a drowned rat.

"He's not here," the guard said. "Check over at the O Unit."

At the O Unit I was told that visiting hours were almost over.

"I came on a bus with three kids over 300 miles, and now you tell me I can't see my husband?" I screamed.

"If you have a complaint, you can go to the Administration Building," the guard said indifferently.

The man in the Administration Office took one look at me trooping in with the three kids, all of us soaked to the skin, and agreed to extend the visiting hours for one hour. It took all the energy I had left to walk back to the O Unit. They searched my purse on the way in.

"Aren't you going to frisk me?" I snapped.

"No, ma'am, This is a minimum security prison. We don't have the same regulations as the other units."

"You mean if I had been told to come here in the first place, I wouldn't have had to go through all this trouble with the dress code?"

He shrugged. I was furious.

Frank was waiting in the visiting room. We sat down at a small table and he leaned over to kiss me. I turned my head and he kissed me on the cheek. The kids were cranky and I felt alienated. The disappointment showed on Frank's face and I wanted to reach over and touch his hand, but I couldn't. I wondered if this was what I had to look forward to for the next 11 years. Now that I finally had gotten in to see him, I couldn't wait to leave. We managed some small talk, but it was awkward for both of us.

The kids were tired and I was grateful when they fell asleep on the bus on the way home. We wouldn't be back in Miami until 11 p.m. and I was exhausted.

"This was your first visit, wasn't it?"

The voice came from the seat acoss the aisle from me. I turned and the woman looked vaguely familiar.

"I saw you in the visitors' line today," she explained. "I can always tell who the first-timers are."

"I really didn't feel like talking and didn't respond, but she just continued on.

"My husband has been in for two years now. After my first visit here, the guards said to him, "You've got a nice-looking wife there. You don't think she's going to wait for you, do you? Taunting, always taunting. They even told him they would work something out so he and I could spend some time alone together. On one condition, of course; that I sleep with them first. They're perverts!"

"The way I look today, I'm sure the guards won't taunt Frank," I said.

"If it's not the guards, it's your husband," she went on. "Every inmate wants his wife to come dressed so he can grab a feel during the visit. With so many people around, the last thing you want to think about is sex. Then, if you don't cooperate, he accuses you of having a jodi."

"A jodi?" I questioned.

"Yeah, the guy who comes in the back door when your husband goes out the front door. My husband actually told me one day that he would forgive me for whatever I might have done. 'What are you talking about?' I said. 'Forgive me for what? Hell, I didn't do nothin'. I was so mad."

"You haven't gone out on him?" I asked.

"I hardly ever leave the house. I live with my parents and spend my time with my two kids. I could put the past two years of my life in a thimble!"

"If it's so hard," I asked, "then why are you waiting?"

"Sometimes I wonder about that myself . . . It isn't easy . . . " Her voice drifted off and we both withdrew into our own thoughts.

For the next week I struggled with the question of whether to wait for Frank. I wanted to do the right thing, but I didn't know what the right thing was. I decided to ask Father Ryan for some advice. He was the priest in the local Episcopal Church I had attended a few times. He had baptized our children. I thought he might be able to help me.

"You need to confront Frank on whether he's going to shape up when he gets out," he said. "If he intends to keep going in the same direction with his life, then it's a waste of your time to wait for him. The church can annul your marriage and you would be free to remarry."

A short time later Frank was temporarily transferred to Dade County Jail in Miami for a few weeks for motions on his case, so I decided to lay out to him what Father Ryan had said.

Dade County Jail is a six-story building and only a limited number of visitors are allowed at a time on each floor. The visiting hours were on Sundays from 1 to 4 p.m. and you could only stay 20 to 30 minutes. Some visitors would stand in line for a couple of hours and never get in because visiting hours would be over before their turn came up. I was not looking forward to another prison visit.

When my turn came, I walked up to the window and showed my identification. I was told to put my purse in one of the lockers along the walls and then the guard pushed the button that opened the steel gates. I walked through into a reception area. It was like walking from one world into another. The chill of the concrete walls and the clang of the steel gates closing tightly behind me made me shudder.

From the reception area, I took an elevator up to the fifth floor where Frank was. A corrections officer was waiting for me when I stepped off the elevator, and I was ushered into an octagon-shaped visiting room.

There was a small, twelve-inch-square window on each of six walls. Each window had a tiny, oval-shaped opening, covered with grating. In order to be heard through it, everyone was shouting to the inmates on the other side. It was hard to talk in all that confusion.

Frank seemed glad to see me and after some small talk I asked, "Frank, do you plan to go straight when you get out? You know, 11 years is a long time to wait, only to have you end up back here."

His expression changed as he said, "Listen, I love you and the kids, but I am who I am. Maybe it would be better if you just got a divorce and went on with your life."

That wasn't what I was hoping to hear. How could he say he loved me and the kids, and yet not be willing to go straight? Didn't he understand I needed a reason to wait? Didn't he have any feelings at all? How could he just dismiss our marriage like that?

It was hard holding back the tears as I left the jail. I felt so confused. I had hoped to come out with a clear answer but I still didn't know.

I was only 22 years old. I loved Frank, but 11 years was a long time. I felt isolated, alone.

Chapter 7

The next few months were a shock. I realized I wasn't prepared for living alone. I had leaned heavily on Frank as my source of security. Despite our stormy relationship, I had depended on him to provide the stability of our home.

Now I felt like a displaced person. I was married, but didn't have a husband. I didn't fit in with single people, because I was married. I was a social misfit. There were a few people around me who tried to help in their own way, but I always felt very much alone.

I was embarrassed about Frank being in prison and kept it from most people. When Michelle, our fourth child, was born I told the hospital staff that Frank had gone on a trip.

I went into labor a few weeks after my visit to Raiford. My mother-in-law came down from Boston to stay with the kids while I was in the hospital. I was really uptight about having this baby because of what the doctor had said about the Inderal possibly causing some damage to the baby.

I was brought to the same hospital where my father lay suffering in the final stages of cancer. The stark reality of life and death loomed before me as I was wheeled into the delivery room and drifted off into frightening, disjointed dreams under the influence of the anesthesia.

When the haze of the anesthesia cleared, a nurse was holding up the baby so I could see her.

"A healthy baby girl," she beamed. "Won't your husband be proud?"

Her words stung; I felt like I didn't have a husband. Later, when I was settled into my hospital room, one of the nurses came in and said, "Your husband is here to see you."

Frank? Here?

In saunters Frank's cousin Joey, carrying on like he's the proud father.

"Oh, our baby's beautiful!" he said, as he flashed a big grin and planted a kiss on my cheek.

Joey is a dark, good looking Italian like Frank and knew he could pass as the father. His eyes sparkled as he winked at me and continued to play the role, hands waving in the air as he expressed his happiness over our beautiful daughter.

My roommate was quite impressed with his enthusiasm. Before he left I whispered to him that I appreciated what he was doing.

A short time later, I was just drifting off to sleep when the nurse came in again, looking bewildered. She cleared her throat and said, "Your husband is here to see you."

Harry, my sister Paula's husband, came bouncing in behind her.

"I just love our baby," he said smiling. "She's got your dark hair and complexion."

The nurse stood there a moment, looking at Harry's blonde hair and blue eyes, then awkwardly left the room. I glanced at my roommate, who gave me a weak smile and then rolled over to face the wall. I was so embarrassed. I think it would have been less humiliating to tell everyone that Frank was in prison.

When I was discharged from the hospital, I was

told that my father was not expected to live much longer.

My sister Paula and I had spent as much time as possible with him over the past few months, caring for him at home while my mother went to work full time.

One day, as I was sitting by his hospital bed, he took my hand and said, "Bunny, what are you going to do when I die? Your mother won't be able to take care of you."

I thought he was referring to finances, but later I realized he meant that she wouldn't be able to cope with my situation.

"Don't worry, I'll be okay, Daddy," I said, fighting back the tears. It touched me deeply that in spite of his own suffering, he was concerned about me.

He soon slipped into a coma, his skin blanched white, his eyes sunk deep into their sockets; he was quickly slipping away. I sat by his side, trying to talk to him in case he could hear and understand in spite of the coma, but often I couldn't say anything at all.

One night my mother, Paula, Billy and I all went together to visit him. My mother entered the room first and began talking to him.

"Bill, the nurse just told us you're getting a new roommate in here tomorrow."

I felt an eerie silence in the room that made me shiver with cold. I looked at my father and noticed his chest wasn't moving. I kept staring at him, waiting for him to take a breath, but he never did. My mother continued her chattering until she noticed the expression on my face. Billy walked over and felt my dad's pulse, while we stood in tense silence.

"He's gone," he said in a low voice.

"Oh, my god, let's get out of here," my mother panicked. She ran out the door and down the corridor, shouting over her shoulder to us, "Hurry up!" She was moving so fast, I had trouble catching up with her.

She calmed down a bit when we got back to the house, but insisted that I make the phone calls to the relatives. She just couldn't handle it.

The next few days were so full of making the funeral arrangements that I didn't feel anything. Even at the wake, when my mother was weeping uncontrollably, I couldn't cry.

My dad had asked that he be buried in Massachusetts. I didn't have the money to go. And what was the point? He was gone anyway.

It wasn't until all the activities were over that his death hit me. I woke up one morning and realized that my security blanket was gone. I cried all day. I felt cheated. I missed him so much.

In my hurt and confusion, I took out my anger on Frank. I wrote him negative letters. I blamed everything on him. All my frustrations came spilling out onto the pages. I accused him of causing all my problems.

As the months dragged on, things got worse. The money quickly ran out.

Everyone demanded their share. They all wanted a piece of the action; the bondsmen, the attorneys. The lawyer's fee for the Adrian Thal case alone was $26,000. And there were other cases and other lawyers. One of the lawyers moved right in on me and let me know how I could pay his fee. I told him to go to hell. I became bitter and resented Frank even more.

I couldn't handle Decor Originals, the company Frank had bought. I decided to sell it. That's when I discovered that Roger had stolen everything but the casting machines. He had been in charge since Frank left. I managed to sell the machines, but the money didn't even cover the bills.

I thought of the money and stolen merchandise we had gone through and how little we had to show for it. There were times Frank had gambled away up to $10,000 in one night and thought nothing of it. I sure could use some of that money now. We just spent it as it came in, with no thought of the future.

Now the checking account was about empty. How could I continue to make the house payments? Maybe I should get a job. But who would watch the kids? The paycheck would be eaten up by baby-sitters.

When a bill arrived in the mail, I sold something in order to pay it. One by one, I sold all the things that once had meant so much to me. My brown mink was worth $2,000; I sold it for $200. One of my diamonds was worth $2,500; I let it go for $250. The pawn shops ripped me off. They wanted to buy everything I had, but didn't want to give me anything for it. I was desperate. I accepted their quick cash deals. I was embittered by the realization that everybody was out to pick the carcass of the family whose husband goes to jail.

One day when my mother was at my house visiting, I sat fidgeting with my engagement ring, thinking, do I have to hock this, too? How much will I get for it? How will Frank feel when he finds out I hocked it? Or will he even care?

"I wish you'd quit that fidgeting, Bunny. You're making me nervous," my mother said.

I couldn't hold back the tears. Wasn't there anyone who understood what I was going through, how I felt? The tears ran silently down my cheeks.

"Why are you crying?" she asked.

"There are payments and bills due, and I can't meet them. I may have to hock my engagement ring and even my wedding band," I said.

After a few minutes of silence, she said in a condescending tone, "Well, why don't you find out what the pawn shop will give you for it, and I'll buy it from you at that price. Then if Frank ever comes home, and you want it back, I'll have it."

How big of you, I thought. But I kept my thought to myself. In the past I had often shared with her the clothes, jewelry and other items that Frank had stolen. Now that I had needs, I couldn't understand why she, in turn, wasn't willing to share with me. The rejection I felt from her intensified.

I was tired of the long, lonely nights and decided I needed to make some changes. If I wanted a social life, then I had to plan it myself. I decided to throw a small party for some friends. Once I invited everyone, I really started to look forward to the evening.

The night of the party I settled the kids into bed early and eagerly waited for everyone's arrival. But the minutes ticked by and no one came. Did my friends consider me a social outcast too? Were they afraid to associate with me? Loneliness, like a damp fog, started to close in around me.

The ringing of the phone startled me.

"Bunny, we're sorry, but we can't come to your house. We were pulling into your driveway tonight and the police stopped us, threatening to arrest us if we went inside. I know they're probably just harassing you, but we can't afford to take the chance of being arrested. I'm sorry . . . "

Was this how it was going to be? I turned on the television set and switched from channel to channel, but there was nothing on but re-runs. I snapped it off and poured myself a drink. The awful fog of loneliness thickened and I went to bed trying to escape, but I couldn't sleep and I just laid there staring at the ceiling.

Driving to the grocery store the next morning, I noticed in my rear view mirror that a police car was following me. They pulled alongside and motioned for me to pull over.

"Let's see your driver's license," the officer said.

I handed it to him and asked, "Why did you stop me? I wasn't speeding."

"We just want to make sure you're not driving without a license," he said.

"Why are you harassing me?" I asked in frustration. "Last night you stopped my friends from coming to my house. Now what are you going to do, stop me every time I pull out of my driveway? You've got Frank in prison; isn't that enough?"

"Oh, we've got Frank in prison where we want him, all right, but we won't be happy until we put you in, too."

As I pulled away from the curb, I thought, Why? What did I do? I don't have a police record. I'm not out robbing people. No more thieves come over to my house; none of that is going on anymore. I'm just trying to make it.

Later that week I got a notice in the mail from the bank, stating that I was three months behind on my house payments and they were beginning foreclosure proceedings.

As things got worse, I realized I was going to have to humble myself and go down to apply for welfare. I had no other alternative.

When the social worker came to visit me, she said that the house was in too classy a neighborhood. "If you want to be on welfare, you'll have to sell the house and move into a different neighborhood," she said.

"Can you get me into federal housing?" I asked.

"Don't plan on it," she said. "The waiting list is a mile long."

"Where am I supposed to find a place big enough for my family that has low rent?" I asked.

She just shrugged her shoulders.

The next day I put the house up for sale. I also decided to sell most of the furniture, thinking I could pay off all my present debts and start over with a clean slate.

The bedroom set sold first. I certainly had no need anymore for a king size bed. I replaced the set with an old one from my mother's house. Half the dresser drawers were warped and wouldn't close all the way, but it would do. I sold the living room set to a friend, who in turn gave me her old sectional couch.

Several months later, the house sold and I made a small profit on it. But the profit was eaten up immediately with all the bills. My house payment had been $165 per month and the only rental I could find was a single family, three bedroom house for $186 per month.

The floors sagged and I soon discovered rats would come through the space between the floor and walls during the night. Twenty-six dollars more per month to live in a dump with scruffy old furniture. It just didn't seem fair.

Then there were the trips to the Miami docks to pick up welfare food for the month: dried beans, flour, cornmeal, instant potatoes. One day as I stood in line waiting for my rationing, I wondered how long it would be before I could afford steak or pork chops again.

Driving home from the docks that day, I decided I

would look for a job under the table and just not report it to welfare. I just couldn't stand living this way.

I applied everywhere I could think of and just when I was about to give up hope of finding anything, Don stopped by the house. He had been my hairdresser for the past four years and my friend, Dottie, worked for him as a wig stylist. She told him that I was having it rough since Frank was gone.

"I need someone to come and work for me," he said, "and Dottie felt you could handle it."

"I'm definitely interested," I said, "but I have to be honest and tell you I have no training as a hairdresser."

"No problem," he said, "I'll have Dottie teach you how to style wigs. It's not that difficult and she said you have a natural flair for it."

"One other problem," I said, "If welfare finds out I'm working, they'll deduct from my check."

"So I'll pay you in cash," he said. "When can you start?"

We agreed that I would start the following week. My sister Paula agreed to babysit Lori and Rocco while I worked. I put Tony in nursery school and found a babysitter just down the street for Michelle.

I didn't like leaving the baby with someone I didn't know, but she seemed pleasant, had four kids of her own, and only charged me $15 per week. I thought that was a good price, considering my hours were from 9 a.m. to 6 p.m.

One morning, before the customers began arriving, Don said to me, "How about going out to dinner with me tonight?"

I was surprised at the invitation and didn't answer right away.

"And we can decide later what to do after dinner," he smirked.

"Thanks, but no thanks," I said and went back to work.

Another day when I was in the back room getting some supplies, he came up behind me and pinched my backside. I slapped him. He was furious. He stalked out of the supply room and was steaming the rest of the day.

He kept trying to hit on me over the next few months and I kept giving him the cold shoulder. When he realized I wasn't going to come across, he made life miserable for me. He insulted me in front of the customers, criticizing my work.

"It's so hard to get decent help these days," he'd say to his clients.

"Bunny! Do this wig over," he'd yell. "This is the most miserable excuse for a hairstyle I've ever seen."

I tried to hide my emotions because I so desperately wanted the job. But often I would burst into tears and run into the back room. I was paying for turning him down. More and more, I looked forward to closing time at 6 p.m. Then, at long last, I could head for home, and some respite.

One day when I stopped to pick up Tony at nursery school on my way home, I was asked to come into the office for a minute.

"Tony tried to throw one of the kids out of a window today," the woman in charge told me. "And yesterday, he tried to break someone's leg. He's a very violent child and we've decided we really don't want him here."

I couldn't believe my ears. What is she talking about? Tony is only three years old. As I looked at her sitting there behind her desk, stiff and unbending, it slowly dawned on me. The news media had been talking a lot about Frank lately. She knew he was suspected of killing someone. Now she thinks we're scum and was accusing Tony of being a juvenile delinquent at age three.

"Fine," I said as I took Tony by the hand. "I'll just find another place for him." I slammed the door as I stalked out.

When I arrived at the babysitter's house to pick up Michelle, a police cruiser was out front, with its light flashing.

"Oh, my god, what's happened now?" I felt a sudden rush of fear and my heart started thumping double-time. I left Tony in the car and went running toward the house. I could hear Michelle screaming as I ran up the sidewalk.

When I got inside, I found her in a bassinet, soaked from head to toe. The room stank of stale urine. I scooped her up in my arms and frantically asked, "What happened?"

The babysitter's husband was just sitting there in a daze, so I turned and directed my question to the police officer.

"His wife took off this morning, left the kids alone, and left a note saying she didn't plan to return," he said. "Apparently, she couldn't cope with the pressures in her life and started using drugs."

How could a mother do that to her kids? I wondered. And what about Michelle? The kids could have taken her outside and dropped her in the lake out back.

When I got home, I called my sister Paula and asked her to bring Lori and Rocco home.

"You won't have to babysit for me anymore," I said. "I'm quitting my job."

The bills continued to pile up. The children were

heckled because their father was a jailbird. Friends awkwardly avoided me because I might ask them for a few dollars for food. Men hit on me because Frank was gone. I felt the stigma of being a social outcast and hated Frank for the pain I was experiencing.

My health wasn't good and I steadily lost weight, going down to 97 pounds. One day I decided to scrape together what money I had to buy some chicken and have a decent supper for a change. I was getting ready to cook it when I remembered I was supposed to return a phone call to my mother. My phone had been disconnected, but my neighbor, Patsy, let me use hers and would take messages for me. I hated to bother her, but she was good about it.

I yelled at Tony to put Baron, our German Shepherd, outside, and told him I was going next door for a few minutes to use the phone. I often thought of getting rid of the dog, but he was like part of the family and the kids really loved him.

When I returned from Patsy's the chicken was no longer on the counter. "Tony!" I yelled, "Where's the chicken?"

He slowly walked into the kitchen with a guilty look on his face. "Where is it?" I demanded.

"Baron was hungry,"

"You let the dog eat the chicken?"

I sat down, put my head in my hands, and wept silently. What would we eat for supper? The cupboards were just about empty. The next day I gave Baron away.

That Christmas, Frank was brought down from Raiford to Dade County Jail to appear in court. On the day of the hearing, I got up and gave each of the kids a piece of toast for breakfast. Things had gotten to the point where all I had left in the house was a loaf of bread, but these were the last four slices. For the past several days I had fed the four kids one meal a day, consisting of one piece of toast each. I hadn't eaten anything in three days.

My welfare check wasn't coming for another week. I only got $130 per month and that was supposed to cover the rent, food and everything. There was no such thing as welfare food stamps in Florida at the time. I just couldn't make ends meet...

My father-in-law contacted me and said that Frank asked him to pick me up and give me a ride to court. He lived nearby, but I seldom saw him. Frank's parents were divorced when he was young and we weren't close to his father. He had a good-paying job and was living with a woman named Helen.

On the way to the court hearing, I said to him, "I don't know what I'm going to do when I get home tonight. There isn't any food in the house for supper."

There was dead silence in the car. Didn't he care about his grandchildren? What did he want me to do, get on my knees and beg him for help? How could he be so cold and hard and selfish?

"You look awful," Helen remarked, after an awkward silence. "Aren't you feeling well?"

"Maybe it has something to do with the fact that I haven't eaten in three days," I snapped.

We drove the rest of the way without speaking.

During the court recess, Frank turned around to talk to me and noticed the strained look on my face.

"Bunny, don't let yourself get so upset about these court cases. I'll be all right."

"Why, you no good s.o.b.," I screamed, "I haven't eaten in three days. I don't give a damn about your going to court!"

Everybody in the courtroom turned and stared at

me. I got up and ran out. My father-in-law followed me and brought me home.

I couldn't stand the tension in the car and finally begged, "Can't you even give me $5 so I can buy food for the kids?"

He didn't answer.

When we stopped in front of the house, he sighed and took $5 out of his wallet.

"Don't feel obligated to pay it back," he said.

As I walked into the house, I missed my dad more than ever.

Chapter 8

It was New Years Day and I was sitting alone by the kitchen table wondering what the new year had in store. The song, "Is That All There Is?", had been floating around in my mind all morning and it was getting to me. I tried to concentrate on other things, but I couldn't. There was only the empty future.

The night before I had let a friend talk me into going to a New Year's Eve Party with her and when the stroke of midnight came, I felt more lonely in that crowd of people than I would have if I had just stayed at home by myself.

I sighed, got up to make myself a cup of coffee, and remembered what my mother had said to me the day before. She wanted to start going to church again and wanted me to go with her. I knew she was lonely, now that my dad was gone. She thought going to church would help somehow.

The only times I had been inside a church in the past few years were on Christmas, and once to have the baby baptized.

"If you come with me, I'll take you out for breakfast afterwards," she said.

That was one way to get a free meal. I just wished she hadn't decided on the 7:30 a.m. mass. I liked to sleep late on Sunday mornings.

As we walked into church and sat down, I noticed

Angel sitting a few rows in front of us. I was surprised to see her here. She was an inmate's wife, too, and the word was that she had become a hooker. The money was a lot better than being on welfare, but I could never bring myself to do that. How could she turn a trick on Saturday night and then show up for church on Sunday morning? Maybe it eased her conscience.

I had trouble concentrating on the sermon. The Priest was a young divinity school graduate who spoke of God in abstract terms. When it was time to take communion, my mother and I just remained seated. We had never made our confirmation and were not allowed to take communion.

On the way out, she talked me into going to the confirmation classes with her. I only agreed because I could see that it was important to her.

The classes were boring and I never understood what the Priest was talking about. I remember my mother getting into an argument with him once about the confessional. She said, "Why should I tell you about my sins, when I can just tell God?" I don't recall his answer, but I know she never went to confession.

On the day of our confirmation, I had to go to the dentist to have an infected tooth pulled. The novacaine wore off while I was in church and I kept feeling like I was going to pass out. One side of my face was all swollen and my whole head ached.

I noticed that as each person stepped forward, the Bishop would give them a slap on the cheek. "If he slaps me on the side I had the tooth pulled, I'll scream," I thought. I lucked out. He slapped the other cheek.

We took communion for the first time, but I didn't see what the big deal was. I didn't feel any different. I wondered why people came back week after week.

After the service, my mother was talking with a friend of hers, but I wasn't in the mood for small talk, so I just smiled and walked past them to the car. My mother told me later that her friend had commented, "Bunny smiles, but her eyes never smile."

I continued to go to church with my mother for a short time, but eventually stopped. What was the point? It sure wasn't helping me any. In fact, things got worse. I never knew where the next meal was coming from; or even if it was coming.

The only things I looked forward to were the occasional weekend visits by Frank's cousin Joey and his wife Angela. He would work around the yard, while Angela helped out with the house and kids. Joey was a clown and could always make me laugh. But they lived quite a distance away and couldn't come very often.

My friend Dottie stopped by when she could and one Saturday said, "Bunny, Rene and I are going to 'Big Daddy's' tonight and want to take you along. It'll be good for you to get out. The old gang is getting together and I know you'd enjoy it."

"But I can't even afford a babysitter," I protested.

"Don't worry about it, we'll pay the babysitter. We'll pick you up around 7 p.m." she said. It would be good to see the old gang again, I thought as I watched her drive away. I missed going to "Big Daddy's", the dancing and the fun.

Dottie and I were sitting in the lounge talking, when she said, "There's Al. Poor guy, he's really feeling down. He was going to marry this girl, and then she cheated on him and got pregnant by another guy. He's having a hard time getting over it. He's such a nice guy, too."

There was an easy confidence and grace about his movements as he sat down at a table and ordered a drink. His brown eyes looked troubled, but there was something solid and secure about him.

He pushed his thick brown hair back from his face and leaned back in his chair. He wore dark brown dress slacks and a white silk shirt. He had just a hint of the forbidden, the playboy about him.

Dottie's husband Rene took her over to the dance floor, so I walked over and introduced myself to Al. His warmth and easy manner made me feel very comfortable and we were soon engrossed in conversation. We danced together a few times and I was aware of how good it felt to be in the arms of a man again.

The evening slipped by quickly and he offered to drive me home. I told him I was with Dottie and Rene and planned to go home with them, but he was persistent and I relented.

When we got to the house, he offered to drive the babysitter home and asked if he could come back afterwards. I told him no. He accepted my answer and didn't hassle me about it. I felt a little twinge of disappointment that he wasn't more persistent. I hadn't realized how hungry I was for affection until he held me in his arms when we were dancing.

The following Saturday I went to the lounge again with Dottie and Rene, hoping Al would be there. He was, and we spent most of the evening together. Once again he drove me home and this time I invited him to come back after he had taken the babysitter home.

At first we just saw each other on Saturday nights, but as our relationship grew, we spent more and more time together.

I felt like I had a new lease on life and even decided to go back to work again. I really needed the money for food and bills, but thought it would be nice to be able to buy some new clothes for myself, too. Don agreed to give me my job back at the Wig Shop. I took it, figuring he wouldn't hassle me now that I was dating Al.

I was ready to start building a new life and was on cloud nine the night Al asked me to marry him. Things were finally coming together for me. I'd have a husband to love and care for me; the kids would have a father. Money won't be so tight with two paychecks coming in and we'll be able to eat well again. We'll be a normal, happy family.

I filed for a divorce and Frank agreed to it. I told my family and friends the good news that Al and I were getting married. But some of them didn't think it was such good news.

They began telling Al, "You're crazy if you think Frank's going to let her go that easy. You're going to end up dead. They'll be scraping you off the sidewalk."

He got nervous about it and was always on edge when we were together. He was terrified that there would be someone lurking in the shadows, waiting for him.

"Al," I said, "Frank's not going to hurt you. He agreed to the divorce and he said he really doesn't care if I get married again."

But he wasn't convinced. He was dealing with Frank's reputation. A strain began to develop between us with all the tension and Al didn't come around to see me for a few weeks.

The next time he came I could see the fear of Frank was still there. We got into an argument and I said, "Stand up for me, you idiot. Frank isn't going to kill you. You've got nothing to worry about. Be a man."

Al was furious. "Be a man? It's me they're going to scrape off the sidewalk – not you!" he shouted. "I think we'd better just forget the wedding plans.

Besides, I was drunk the night I asked you. I didn't know what I was saying."

"Just get out of here," I said in a low, cold voice.

After he left, it began to rain and I went outside, looking up at the dark, gray sky. The rain beating down from the clouds mingled with the tears on my face. That damp fog of loneliness enveloped me once more.

I began taking anti-depressant drugs to get through the day. I took sleeping pills to get through the night. I had trouble coping with the kids. Don increased his pressure on me at work. Financially, I wasn't able to make ends meet.

My mother-in-law sensed the state I was in, even at a distance, and offered to take Lori and Rocco for a while to ease the pressure on me. I put them on the plane to Boston one morning, picked up a bottle of Old Crow on the way home, and spent the rest of the day drinking.

I remember staring at the walls for hours, taking a sleeping pill and then another, then a drink, trying to sleep. But sleep wouldn't come. An awful depression draped my life like a cold wet blanket. Weekends at Big Daddy's Lounge became a blur. I would watch for Al, but he was hardly ever there. I remember sitting at the bar one night seeing faces float around in front of me. I felt like I was losing my mind.

I started out each morning with a couple of drinks before going to work; when I got home, I would feed the kids, put them to bed, and drink until I fell asleep. The next day the routine would be the same. Days turned into weeks and weeks into months. I hardly noticed.

One day while I was at work, the social worker from welfare stopped by and asked my neighbor where I was. She told her I was working. That week I received a notice that I had to report my income to welfare so it could be deducted from my check, or quit working. I quit working.

Whenever the edge of the alcoholic haze would clear, the depression became unbearable, so I drank even more.

My friend Dee stopped by one day and said, "Bunny, what's wrong with you? Why can't you get your act together?"

"Wrong?" I said, "What could be wrong?" My voice turned sarcastic. "Everything's just fine."

"Bunny, come on, look around you. The house is a mess. There's sugar spilled all over the kitchen floor, and dirty dishes all over the counters. The kids are tearing the house apart, and you just sit there. How can you say there's nothing wrong?"

I didn't answer, but just sat there feeling numb, and staring into space. Eventually she gave up and left.

That night Al stopped by. I hadn't seen him for quite a while and it took me by surprise. I began screaming at him, "What the hell are you doing here? You already told me you never loved me. Isn't that enough?"

"I came by to see if you were okay," he said.

"What's it matter to you if I'm okay . . . you don't really care. Nobody gives a damn," I shouted.

He just stood there, looking at me. I was suddenly very conscious of how I looked. My black hair was dirty and plastered in wet ringlets around my face. My eyes were red-rimmed from too much booze and too little sleep.

"Get out!" I screamed, throwing the drink in my hand across the room. The glass shattered against the wall and the contents splattered everywhere. "Get out!"

My heart started racing so I took a couple of pills

to slow it down. Then I took several sleeping pills and crawled into bed without bothering to undress. I didn't care if I ever woke up again.

I fell into a short, fretful sleep and woke up in a gray void. I reached over in a daze and took more pills.

"Please, God, just let me sleep . . . "

When I woke up again, it was daylight. Great waves of nausea swept over me. I managed to get out of bed, but my body was uncoordinated and I stumbled about. Somehow I made it to my neighbor's house and asked to use the phone.

I called my mother, but my speech was slurred and I knew I wasn't making sense. I dropped the phone and put my head down on the table. I couldn't even cry.

My neighbor picked up the phone and I heard her saying, "I don't know what's wrong with her, but you'd better get over here right away." Her voice sounded far away.

My mother and sister Paula arrived, along with my Aunt Dee and cousin Joey. I wondered what they were doing here. They brought me home and tried to get me to eat something, but I was having trouble finding my mouth. Then they forced me to drink strong, black coffee. I threw up all over myself.

Paula said, "Come on, Bunny, I'll help you into the bathroom and give you a bath."

"I can take care of myself," I yelled as I jerked away from her and stumbled towards the bathroom.

When I didn't come out for a while, Paula came into the bathroom and found me sitting nude in the tub, with no water. I asked her for a towel so I could dry off. She didn't know whether to laugh or cry. My mother came into the bathroom and flushed all my pills down the toilet, while Paula cleaned me up and helped me get dressed.

"Maybe if she got away for a while, she would feel better," my mother said to Auntie Dee, pacing the floor and wringing her hands.

"We'll take care of her," Auntie Dee answered.

"Good, I've got to get back to work," my mother said, relieved.

"You don't give a damn about me, do you?" I screamed at my mother. "Your work is more important than I am!"

She turned and said with disgust in her voice, "Oh, Bunny, that's not true," and walked out the door.

Auntie Dee helped Paula get the two kids, Tony and Michelle, dressed and into the car, while Joey helped me. "You can stay with us for a while," Auntie Dee said. "You need some rest."

I blanked out when I got into the car, and didn't remember anything until the next day. It took me a while to figure out where I was and how I got there. The house was quiet. Everybody must still be sleeping. I was totally exhausted, but couldn't sleep anymore.

I didn't want to think, but couldn't stop the hopeless flow of dark thoughts. My life was a big nothing, a vacuum. It wasn't worth taking up any space. What was there to live for anyway? Did anybody really care if I lived or died? My dad would have cared, but he was gone.

The black void within me increased to the point of being unbearable. I stumbled out of bed and groped my way to the bathroom. I caught a glimpse of my reflection in the mirror. There were dark hollows under my eyes, my hair was matted and needed shampooing. I felt and looked like I was 90 years old.

I opened the medicine cabinet, but it was empty. Not even an aspirin. My aunt must have hidden everything. I was frantic and began searching everywhere for some pills, anything to put me out of this misery. But I found nothing.

I staggered into the living room and collapsed in a corner of the sofa. I cried myself to sleep.

The next two weeks are almost totally blocked out of my memory. I was only vaguely aware of the activities in the house. I realized my mother-in-law had arrived from Boston with Lori and Rocco. She thought having the children around me would help, but I was too weak to care and I spent all my time sleeping, oblivious to what was going on.

When I started feeling a little stronger, my mother-in-law took me and the four kids back to my house and agreed to stay until I felt ready to handle things on my own again. I took advantage of her being there and let her take full care of the house and the kids.

As soon as I felt strong enough to go out, I lied to her and told her I was going job hunting. Instead, I went out drinking and came home high as a kite. I decided as long as she was there to babysit, I'd just go out whenever I could, with whomever I could get to go with me.

One night I met a psychiatrist in a bar and dated him several times, thinking this is just what I need . . . some free counseling. I noticed that he didn't drink much and didn't seem to like it that I did. It made me uncomfortable. One night he took a highball out of my hand and said, "Bunny, you've got to stop drinking. I know what I'm talking about, and you're well on your way to becoming an alcoholic."

I could tell by the concerned look on his face that he was dead serious. I lay awake all night thinking about it. I knew he was right. I had to get my act together. I decided to start the next day without a drink, although the thought of facing the day without it terrified me.

I managed to stop the drinking, but couldn't face life without popping pills. I continually increased the dosage, until my supply ran out. The doctor refused to give me a prescription more than twice a month.

I was panic-stricken. I went to my brother Billy, begging him to make a connection for me with a pusher. I knew he was smoking pot and popping pills himself. He refused.

When I came home my mother-in-law was waiting to talk to me. I knew she was disgusted with me.

"Bunny, you've got a rotten attitude, and if you don't get yourself together, and quick, I'm going back to Boston. I'm not putting up with this much longer."

Her words stung me. She was the only stable factor in my life. If I lost her, who would be left? I worked at being more considerate, but I was so strung out, I just couldn't seem to help myself. One day, true to her word, she packed up and left.

I wasn't fully aware of how I had neglected my responsibilities until she left. Now there was no one but me to take care of the house and the kids, and they needed me desperately.

I made up my mind to stop taking the pills and the next few weeks were torture. I had insomnia. I was sick and had to fight depression continually. At times I felt as if I were losing my mind. Somehow I got through it and felt a sense of victory when it was over.

But the feeling didn't last for long. It was just a short while later that I received an eviction notice from my landlord, because I owed several months back rent. I had no money and didn't know what to do. I contacted the Welfare office to see if they could help.

"Can't you move in with some relatives?" the social worker asked.

"No," I said. "We were just told that my mother

has Hodgkins Disease and my sister and her family are moving down from Massachusetts into her house to take care of her. There's not room for me and my four kids in that small house."

"There must be another relative that could take you in," she said.

"With four kids? I'm telling you, there's no place for me to go," I said.

"Well, I don't really know how we can help you," she said.

"But what am I supposed to do? The only thing I have is an old car; am I supposed to live in that with four kids?"

"Well, let us know how you make out," she said as she hung up the phone.

Once again I felt my world begin to crumble around me. Just when I would think I was gaining ground, everything would collapse. In spite of my efforts, I was getting nowhere.

Chapter 9

After serving two years in Raiford State Prison, Frank got transferred down to Glades Correctional Institute in Belle Glade, Florida. Instead of a 300-mile trip to visit him, it would now be 70 miles. We had continued sporadic correspondence with each other the past two years, even though I hadn't been visiting him. I sensed in his recent letters that he was going through some internal changes.

Another inmate's wife, whose husband was also in the Glades, contacted me and asked if I would like to travel with her to Belle Glade and share the gas expense. I decided to go along. I made several Sunday visits at the prison with Frank.

On one of those visits, Frank greeted me enthusiastically.

"I've got something to tell you," he said. "I've converted."

I just stared at him and thought, "Oh, my god, he's been in prison too long; he's going to tell me he's become a queer."

"Converted into what?" I asked as calmly as I could.

"I got saved," he said.

I didn't know what he was talking about. He began to tell me how he had gone through this time of questioning about his life and had talked with Chaplain Max Jones about it. Max had prayed for him and he had experienced the presence of God. He had cried and cried down on his knees and felt bathed in God's love.

Frank cry? I couldn't quite imagine that.

"Bunny, I'm going to live different now," he continued. "Jesus is real and He touched me. I've changed on the inside."

He seemed genuinely excited, but I still didn't understand what he was talking about. Then I thought, maybe it will help him get parole, maybe that's his angle.

"Well, that's nice, Frank," I said.

He was disappointed with my response. The next time I went back, he was still excited and talked about his experience and how great the Bible studies were with Max Jones and the guys. I didn't understand and just watched him carefully. I figured he would do anything to get out of prison.

Our visits were fairly pleasant and we began to build a relationship together again. Because of Frank's conversion to Christianity, he now felt that God meant for us to do what we could to put our marriage back together again. I looked forward to the visits, but was afraid to let my feelings toward him surface again. I had been hurt too many times.

One morning I received a call from Judge Harris. He was a former judge that Frank had known for a long time, and he had a great deal of political clout. "I'm driving up to see Frank tomorrow," he said.

"Why?" I asked curiously.

"It's business," he said. "Would you like to go along?" he asked.

"Yes, I'll go. What time will you leave?" I asked, wondering what the "business" was all about.

"I'll pick you up at 9 a.m.," he said.

We were given the cook's tour of the whole prison. It was a big deal for a circuit court judge to be there. Then we went to the Chaplain's office and we were allowed to visit alone with Frank.

"Frank, a couple of your friends are willing to put up the money necessary for you to get a parole," said Harris. "All you have to do is acknowledge that you owe them the $10,000 back, and you can be home for Christmas."

Home for Christmas? I couldn't believe it. I had forgotten the pull that Judge Harris had. Why, $10,000 is a drop in the bucket. Frank could easily steal that much in one night, pay them back, and he'd never have to steal again.

I was so excited, I got up and threw my arms around Frank. I could feel his body was tense.

"Judge, what I'm about to say, my wife might think is very cruel," Frank said.

I couldn't imagine what he would say that I would think was cruel.

"Judge, I thank you for your interest in me and my family. But I'm a Christian now."

The judge looked startled.

"For the first time in my life," Frank said, "I have peace of mind, and I'd rather do every day of those 22 years with Jesus, than to walk out of here and leave Him behind."

"Tell my friends I said thank you, but no thank you."

I couldn't believe he turned it down! I thought he'd do anything to get out of prison! Why didn't he take the Judge up on the offer? I hardly spoke to the Judge on the ride home. He attempted some small talk, but neither of us wanted to discuss what Frank had said.

My thoughts went round and round during the next

few days. How could Frank give up a chance at parole? Why did he turn down his freedom? He used to always talk about escaping or buying off the Parole Board. I knew he wanted out. And yet, he turned it down. Could it be that his experience with God was real?

On the next visit, I told Frank all the financial trouble I was having, the eviction notice, etc. I could tell he really felt bad for me, but didn't expect him to say, "Let's pray about it."

"Right here, in the visitor's park?"

He began praying and I felt so embarrassed. I wished I hadn't told him anything.

I kept my eyes open and watched him. I was hoping the people around us would think we were just talking. He prayed as though God was right there with us and I noticed the tears running down his cheeks. I still didn't understand what was happening, but whatever it was, it was real for Frank.

He invited me to come to the chapel services, where he would share his testimony. I taped it and passed the tape around to some of our friends to listen to.

"When he gets out, he'll change and go right back to the old Frank," they said.

One friend laughed and said, "He'll probably become a preacher, just so he can use his clerical collar as a disguise for his stickups."

Another said, "If Frank's a Christian, then I'm a nun."

All of their comments upset me and I talked to Frank about it.

"Don't worry about it, Bunny," he said. "When I get out and start living it, they'll see that it's real. There's nothing else you can do about it right now."

He wasn't upset at all.

I began to attend chapel services at the prison regularly, but I felt uncomfortable. I especially hated the altar calls at the end. I'd watch people go forward for prayer and think, "They're making a spectacle of themselves. I'll never do that."

After a while, I stopped attending the services and just made excuses to Frank about why I couldn't be there on time for chapel. I showed up when it was over.

As our visits continued, I began to realize that the change in Frank was real. Our relationship was changing, too. We didn't argue like we used to, and he was more sensitive to my feelings. If God could change Frank, I wondered, then could He help me? I felt like I had already tried church and it hadn't worked. But Frank said it had nothing to do with church; it was a personal experience. That had to come first; then church would come alive.

Frank certainly prayed differently than I was used to hearing. He believed God was right there with him, and he just talked to Him. I used to say my prayers at night, but it was just a habit. It didn't really mean anything. I always felt that God was way up there in space someplace, the devil was way down below somewhere, and here I was somewhere in between.

I finally decided that whatever it was that Frank had, I wanted it too, even though I didn't understand it. I started attending the chapel services again, but couldn't bring myself to go forward for the altar call.

One afternoon at home, I went into my bedroom and got down on my knees. I felt really awkward. The kids were outside playing and it was quiet in the house. I was nervous, because I didn't know what was going to happen to me.

"Dear Jesus," I prayed, "Please come into my life, like You did in Frank's." I felt shaky as I got up off my knees and was glad it was over.

The next Sunday I told Frank what I had done and that I was disappointed that I didn't have a dramatic experience like his. I thought maybe it didn't take, because I didn't cry.

"God works different ways with different people, Bunny," Frank said. "I'm sure He heard your prayer and accepted it."

I continued to feel uncomfortable during the altar call in the chapel. Part of me would feel it was okay that I had prayed at home, but the other part of me would think, "Yeah, you did it at home because you were too ashamed to go up front and give your life to God in front of other people." I felt like I had cheated and gotten salvation through the back door.

I began to watch Billy Graham on television and would cry through the whole altar call, when I saw all those people going forward to give their lives to God. There was certainly a growing awareness in me that it was real.

My friends would still stop by from time to time and invite me out to the lounges, but I no longer had a desire to go.

"Life is different for me now, and I'm uncomfortable going there," I told them.

Chaplain Max Jones got special permission to take Frank and some of the other Christian inmates to Dunklin Memorial Camp in Okeechobee, Florida, to sing and share their testimonies at the church service there. Frank told me when they were going, so that I could spend the day there, too. I drove down with several other inmates' wives.

Their church service at the camp was very informal compared to what I was used to. People were smiling and clapping their hands to the music, some had their hands raised in the air. I enjoyed the music, but didn't participate in the hand clapping.

Security was not tight while the men were at the camp, and we were allowed to wander around the grounds after the service. I noticed several inmate couples heading in the direction of the orange groves.

Frank took my arm grinning, and said, "Come on, let's go for a walk."

I was happy that he was so enthusiastic about being able to spend some time alone with me. As we neared the orange groves, however, I realized he had more in mind than just walking and talking.

The couples scattered in all directions and settled down under the orange trees. I was a bit tense, thinking of a snake possibly crawling on top of us.

The men were invited back to the camp many times. It was one of their favorite places to go. After every service someone would say, "Hey Frank, why don't you go for a walk in the orange groves?"

"That's a great idea," Frank would say, and off we'd go. Those were fertile groves.

Financially, things were not getting any better at home and the day of my eviction was approaching rapidly. I knew I couldn't postpone it much longer. Frank told Chaplain Max Jones about it and he offered to help me find a place to live near his family. I really didn't like the idea of moving to a new community where I didn't know anyone and the kids would have to change schools, but felt I had no choice. And to top it off, I had just discovered that I was pregnant.

Max made arrangements for me to move into a federal housing project. I comforted myself with the thought that at least I wouldn't have so far to drive to visit Frank.

The day I moved, some people from one of the churches came over to see if I needed some help unpacking. Apparently Chaplain Jones had told them about me. I thought it was nice of them to stop by. One of them introduced himself as one of the elders of the church.

"How many niggers do you think it will take for you to unpack?" he asked.

I just looked at him and said, "What?"

"How many niggers do you think you'll need to get the boxes unpacked and things straightened up?" he repeated.

How many niggers do I need? I couldn't believe a Christian would talk that way.

"That's okay," I said, "I can unpack by myself."

"No, I'm going to pay for a couple of niggers to come over here and do it for you," he said as he left with the others.

A short time later, two black women came and got everything unpacked and cleaned up. I didn't have to do anything. Then some other people from the church came by and brought me some fresh vegetables and paid my first month's rent. At least I would be able to eat and have a secure roof over my head.

The first night I slept there, every sound woke me up. There was a plane that kept flying low over the house and I was sure it was going to crash. Later I found out they were just spraying the sugar cane fields.

Michelle and Rocco both ended up in the hospital soon after we moved; Michelle with a virus, and Rocco with an infection he picked up through a cut on his forehead. His whole face was swollen and disfigured.

The first Sunday in town, I went to church and

noticed that everyone was dressed in suits and ties and fancy dresses, including the children. I looked at how we were dressed, and felt uncomfortable.

Part way into the service I realized that the Pastor was calling on people at random to lead in prayer. I had never prayed out loud in front of anybody in my whole life and I was terrified he was going to call on me. I was so relieved when the service was over.

That week I decided to look for a job. I didn't like being in the house all day and I needed the extra money. It was impossible to make ends meet with my welfare check. I applied in several places, but found nothing. When I visited Frank and told him about it, he didn't like the idea.

"You belong home with the kids," he said. "And maybe you shouldn't be taking money under the table anymore."

I got angry with him. After all, he got fed three square meals a day in prison. I was the one out in the world trying to struggle and make it with four kids. If I felt like getting a job, I'd get one. I was used to making my own decisions now. He just didn't understand what it was like out here.

A strain developed between us over this.

That's when Paul stepped into my life. He worked on the maintenance crew in the federal housing project I was living in. Shortly after I moved in he came over to do some painting in the house.

He was a few years younger than I, and was tall and slender, with a boyish face and a contagious grin. He stood in the doorway holding a paint bucket in one hand, running his other hand through his blonde hair. His blue eyes sparkled as he introduced himself and explained why he was there.

We talked and joked while he painted. It felt good to have someone to talk to and have a little fun with. I had so little fun in my life, it seemed. After he left each day I would feel a twinge of guilt about enjoying his company so much, but then I brushed it aside.

When we talked seriously one day, he told me he was separated from his wife and planned to get a divorce. I told him I could understand what he was going through and told him a little about my stormy relationship with Frank. I invited him to stay for dinner that night and we continued our conversation. After dinner he played with the kids for a while, tucked them into bed for me, and then left.

I knew I would miss him when his work was done at the house. On his last day I walked him to the door and he looked at me through the clearest light blue eyes I'd ever seen. I was in his arms before I realized what was happening, and he was kissing me.

I cried after he left. My emotions had me totally confused. How could I be falling in love with Paul when my relationship with Frank was being restored?

A few nights later Paul showed up at the door. He was dressed very casually in faded jeans and a blue work shirt with rolled-up sleeves. His blonde hair was freshly shampooed and his light blue eyes were even more devastating with the pale blue of his shirt.

I invited him in. He was carrying a guitar.

"I didn't know you played guitar," I said.

"Oh, I just kind of mess around with it," he said. "I don't really play all that well."

"Play something for me," I said, settling into a chair.

He began to play "As Tears Go By."

"That's one of my favorite songs," I said.

"Then why don't you sing along while I play?"

I began to sing, "It is the evening of the day, I sit and watch the children play, smiling faces I can see, but none for you and me . . . I sit and watch as tears go by . . . ''

I choked up and couldn't finish the song.

Paul put down the guitar and asked, "What's wrong, Bunny?"

"The words just got to me," I said, the tears filling my eyes.

"Come over here and sit next to me," he said.

I curled up next to him on the couch and he put his arms around me.

"You know, Bunny, I really care about you."

We sat in silence for a while and I just enjoyed the comfort and closeness I felt.

Then he said, "Hey, go get a deck of cards and we'll play a game of Rummy. This rebel is going to beat your tail off in a game of cards."

"Not a chance," I said. "We Yankees beat you once, and this one is going to do it again."

"Oh really? You city slickers think you're pretty good, don't you?" he laughed.

I got out the cards and we spent the evening joking and teasing each other about his southern and my northern background.

Before he left, he asked me out to dinner for Friday night and I accepted.

The next day I splurged and went out and bought myself a new outfit to wear.

When he picked me up on Friday night he said, "You look terrific, Bunny."

"Thanks," I smiled.

"You know, you really are beautiful," he said, as he opened the car door for me.

He took me to an elegant seafood restaurant and we had a quiet candlelight dinner. Afterwards he drove down to the ocean and we walked on the beach in the moonlight.

"Bunny, you know, I really love you," he said as we walked hand in hand.

"I think I'm falling in love with you, too." I said.

He took me in his arms and kissed me. It was a perfect evening.

When I visited Frank, there was tension between us. I found myself arguing with him over little things. I was torn between Frank and Paul. Each one met different emotional needs in my life. Frank was strong and I had always been able to lean on him. Paul was easygoing and brought some fun into my life. He never argued with me. He was always kind and was able to lift me up out of my bad moods.

I continued attending church on Sundays and even went to prayer meetings on Wednesday nights. I felt like a hypocrite. I had made a commitment to Christ, but wasn't conforming to this new way of life.

Sunday, sitting in church, my thoughts flashed back to Angel, the hooker I had seen in church the year before when I went with my mother. I was no better than she was. I knew I had to make a decision and so I sat down and wrote Frank a letter telling him about Paul and my love for him. I wanted Frank to hear it from me first. I asked him for a divorce.

When I told Paul about writing the letter to Frank, he said, "Why did you do that?"

"I can't be visiting Frank on Sundays and seeing you during the week," I said. "I had to make a decision."

"Let's talk about this later, Bunny. I have to think through some things."

The rest of the evening had an uneasiness about it. After Paul left, some of the sureness about my decision came into question.

I decided to go visit Frank again that week. On my way back home I thought, "What am I doing? Frank is helpless to fight for me because he's in prison. He believes God wants our family restored, and I'm ruining all that. How could I do that to him?

But when I got back to the house Paul was waiting for me and I suppressed my thoughts. I just went through the motions of living that week.

I went to church that Sunday as usual, but I couldn't concentrate on the sermon. When Max Jones stood up and sang the altar call, suddenly all the guilt I had been carrying came rushing to the surface and I knew I had to go forward to pray.

I brushed past the woman sitting next to me, saying, "Please get out of the way. I need to go down to the altar." I got down on my knees and poured my heart out.

"Oh, God, I've been deceived. My whole life is just in shambles. I told the kids they were going to have a new daddy. I made the wrong decision. I'm so sorry. You're my last hope. If you don't help me, then it's all over for me. Please forgive me."

I stayed there on my knees a long time, allowing the tears to do their cleansing. when I got up to leave, I felt different. Clean. Like I had been washed on the inside. Peace replaced the turmoil within.

I went back to the house and called Paul. I told him what happened to me in church and said our relationship would have to end because it was all wrong. He was quiet. I told him I was giving my notice to the housing authority the next morning, that I was leaving. "You're not really going to leave, Bunny," he said. I could tell he didn't believe me, but that didn't matter.

After I hung up I was relieved. My decision was made. I knew everything was over between Frank and me, too. How could I expect him to forgive me for this? My thoughts went back to the time Frank had prayed with me that our marriage would be bound in heaven. It didn't look like our marriage was going to be bound anywhere. I cried far into the night.

The next morning I notified welfare and the federal housing authority that I was moving. I wrote Frank a letter, explaining why I was leaving, and that my plan was to go to Boston and stay with his mother for a while. I told him I would understand if he didn't want to write back.

While I was packing to leave, Paul stopped by. It was then I found out that he wasn't separated from his wife. He hadn't planned to get a divorce, like he had said. He told me she was pregnant and he was looking forward to having a child. He said he still loved me, however, and asked me to stay so we could continue to see each other.

How could I have been so gullible? I had believed everything he told me. I made it clear it was over between us and that I wouldn't be coming back. His visit confirmed to me that I was making the right decision.

I sold what furniture and belongings I could, and just gave the rest away. I left for Boston feeling more in control of my own life than I ever had before.

After I had been in Boston a while, I received a card and letter from Frank. He said he had been in the hospital with the flu and apologized for not writing sooner, but he didn't say anything about our relationship or what happened with Paul.

I wrote him back and asked if he thought there was still a chance that we could work things out together. I waited every day for the mail to come with his reply.

He wrote back, saying we both should just forget

the past and be willing to look ahead and make a fresh start.

A fresh start? Was that possible after what we'd both been through over the past years?

I wanted to believe it was, more than anything. Then I recalled a verse that Max Jones had shared once:

"When someone becomes a Christian, he becomes a brand new person inside. He is not the same anymore. A new life has begun." II Corinthians 5:17. – Living Bible.

God wasn't interested in the reasons my life was a mess, nor did He think I could undo everything I had done. I'd often thought if I could only start over knowing what I know now, I'd do things different. Well, that's what God has promised me – new life, and I'm going to trust Him for it.

Chapter 10

I remained in Boston during the summer of 1971. I attended a small church where the Pastor and members were very friendly and made me feel accepted.

Frank and I continued to write, sharing our hopes and dreams for the future, piecing our relationship back together. The highlight of my day was the arrival of the mailman, delivering Frank's latest letter.

I remember the day his letter came saying that he might be up for early parole in October and would be going on work-release soon in Kissimmee, 220 miles north of Miami. It was more than I had hoped for. I had thought I would have to wait another seven years.

I called my sister Paula at my mother's in Miami and she said I could stay with her until Frank found us a place to live. I immediately made reservations to fly to Miami with the kids. It was August and I could hardly believe that Frank would be out in a few months and we would begin our new life together.

Captain McCall, the head of the work-release center, gave Frank permission to go out after work hours to look for a house to rent. He found one on Alligator Lake in St. Cloud, but was only making minimum wage on the construction job, and I wondered how we would be able to furnish a whole house. I had gotten rid of everything except our clothes.

Then Frank heard about a job one night per week at a local auction and got permission to take it. He watched the furniture that came through and managed to buy all the basics we needed for about $100. It was certainly not the type of furniture we had been accustomed to years before, but it would do.

My mother gave me her old set of pots and pans and my aunt gave me some odds and ends of dishes so that we could get by.

Frank's mother agreed to fly down from Boston, to help me get settled into the house in St. Cloud, and stay with me until Frank got out on parole. I was nearing the end of my pregnancy and she would take care of the kids while I went to the hospital to have the baby.

To save money, Ma Costantino was flying in on a late flight arriving at 1 a.m. Halloween night. My friends, Dee and Ramona were visiting my sister Paula and me that night at my mother's house in Hialeah. They decided to come along for the ride to Miami International Airport. We all piled into Paula's old Chevy and set out.

Paula was a year younger than me, and like me had ebony black hair, dark eyes and complexion typical of someone of Armenian descent. She was not quite five feet tall and looked comical, leaning forward peering through the steering wheel as she drove.

Dee and Ramona could have passed for our sisters. They had long black hair and dark complexions.

I looked forward to my mother-in-law coming down. She was like a second mother to me and her presence had given me a sense of stability in the past four years.

She got off the plane and headed toward us with the determined stride that was so characteristic of her. She was wearing her customary black cotton housedress and her gray hair was pulled back into a French twist.

We all greeted her warmly, and after picking up her luggage, headed towards Hialeah. Dee and Ramona were in the back seat and I sat in the middle of the front seat, between Ma and Paula.

We were crossing the canal that separates Miami Springs from Hialeah and came to a stop on the bridge, waiting for the traffic light to change. Ma, who was hard of hearing, was telling us that the plane flight had bothered her ears and they kept popping. Because of it, she was having trouble hearing, even out of her good ear.

"Paula, would you put your window up part way?" Dee said. "My hair is blowing in my face."

"Vanity, vanity," Paula teased as she rolled her window part way up.

Suddenly a sound went off in my head. Weeee-oooop. Everything went black. We must have been in an accident, I thought. But the car hadn't moved. My sight returned almost immediately, but I was having trouble holding my head up.

Paula said, "Somebody broke my window."

I reached up to feel the back of my head and my hand felt wet. I looked down and my light blue maternity top was splattered with blood. I started screaming and buried my face in my mother-in-law's arms. Paula quickly pulled off the bridge and into a nearby gas station, but it was closed and no one was around.

She turned to see if Dee and Ramona were all

right. They were just sitting there, staring straight ahead, with a glazed look. Paula started yelling, "Dee! Ramona! Are you all right?"

Dee snapped out of it and said haltingly, "Yeah, I'm okay." Ramona just sat there. "She's okay too," Dee said. "We just have broken glass on us."

Then Dee noticed the blood oozing down the back of my head. "Paula, we'd better get to the hospital, and fast!"

Even though there was no traffic at that time of night, Paula kept stopping at the traffic lights.

"Paula, please, there's no cars coming. Just keep moving!"

Paula slammed on the brakes when we arrived at the hospital and we all tumbled out. My mother-in-law held me up while I staggered toward the Emergency Entrance.

"You know, Ma," I said, "that couldn't have been a rock that broke the window. I'm soaked with blood. It must have been a bullet."

I felt her body tense up. "Bunny, don't even say that," she said.

In the Emergency Room my vision was not normal. I could see people's heads and legs, but their whole chest area was blanked out.

By then my hair and maternity clothes were drenched with blood. The dizziness increased and I knew my legs weren't going to support me much longer. The interns and nurses just stood there staring at me.

"Don't just stand there. Do something!" Ma Costantino shouted.

They scrambled to help me into one of the treatment rooms. A foreign intern began asking me my name and other information.

"Did you call the police?" he asked.

"Call the police? When have I had time to call the police?" I asked.

He brought me to X-ray and when I returned, the police were at the hospital. I was left alone in the treatment room.

The bullet must be lodged in my brain. I just knew I wouldn't make it through surgery.

"Please, God," I prayed, "Let me live long enough to watch my children grow up. They've been through so much already. They've been without a dad for the last four years and now to lose a mother."

In the other room the police were asking my mother-in-law, "Did you hear the sound of a gun go off or anything?" "How could I?" she said. "I'm deaf in one ear and can't hear out of the other."

They thought she was being smart and asked Paula, "Who is this old lady anyway?"

"Who are you calling an old lady?" Ma shouted, raising herself up to her full five-foot frame in front of the six-foot cop. "My name is Anna Costantino!"

He backed off and began questioning the others.

"Were you followed?" he said. "Do you have any idea who did it? Did Bunny have a boyfriend? Do you think Frank set this up? Isn't he getting out soon?"

"Shouldn't you be out looking for the lunatic who did this, instead of standing around asking us these damn-fool questions?" Ma flared.

"The way I see it, Frank might have set this up," he said. "She must have a boyfriend. She's obviously pregnant and Frank's still in prison," he smirked.

"Frank is the father of that child," she said indignantly.

"How could that be possible?" he retorted.

"It's none of your damn business, you fresh monkey cop!" she shouted.

"This really frosts me," Dee said. "Bunny's

laying in there with a bullet in her head and all you cops care about is trying to pin it on Frank."

"The thing that bothers me most," Ramona said quietly, "is that they don't seem to care about Bunny at all."

Dr. Fields arrived and came into the treatment room where I was laying. "You're a very lucky lady," he said. "The X-rays show that the bullet traveled just under the skin, but didn't crack the skull. Your vision will return to normal once we remove the bullet."

After being stitched up, I insisted on going home. Paula had called my brother Billy and he had just arrived. My mother-in-law and I rode home with him; Dee and Ramona rode with Paula.

Ma climbed into the back seat and I laid down on the front seat. I was taking no chances. There was that ever-present fear that another bullet might come smashing through the window.

Billy said, "The police told me they searched Paula's car and found the other part of the .38 caliber bullet in the back seat on the floor. The bullet hit the edge of the partially rolled-up window and split. They said if it hadn't hit the window like that, someone's head would have been blown off." Thank goodness for Dee's vanity, I thought. And Paula didn't get hit because she was so short.

It bothered me that the police suspected Frank. He still had a reputation to live down. It's funny, they didn't even bother questioning me. I would have told them he did not do it.

When we got to the house, I called my mother who was caring for a sick aunt in Massachusetts. I told her I had been shot, but was okay.

"I'll get on the first flight back to Miami," she said, and she was back the next day.

Several days after the shooting I was watching the 11 p.m. news on television when the phone rang.

"My car broke down and I need someone to come get me." It was my brother Billy.

Mother had fallen asleep on the couch, and I woke her up. "Billy just called," I said. "His car broke down and he needs you to go get him."

She was irritated that I woke her up. "Bunny, just go get him yourself," she snapped.

Me? I wasn't going to leave the house. What if somebody tried to shoot me again? What if this time I wasn't so lucky? I looked down at my mother as she just rolled over and closed her eyes.

"*Why* doesn't she go? How can she be so *insensitive*?"

"Calm down, Bunny," I said to myself. "This is stupid. You can't stay in the house for the rest of your life. Besides, the police claim it was just a freaky Halloween prank. There's nobody out there trying to kill you. Why should you take this out on your mother?"

She was already asleep. I stood there looking at her. She wasn't responsible for the way I felt.

I picked up my purse and headed for the door, knowing it was time to get out, to leave Miami and its bad times behind me. It was no longer a friendly home for me.

Chapter 11

As soon as I was well enough, Paula helped me pack a U-Haul and we drove to St. Cloud. She stayed long enough to help me unpack, then headed back home.

I was tired from all the unpacking and went into the bedroom to rest. When I laid down on the bed, the soft, lumpy mattress almost swallowed me up. I laughed at the sight of my head and feet suspended in air, while my bottom was just about on the floor.

My thoughts went back to the king size electric bed we used to have. I was more content now in the lumpy mattress than I ever was with all that luxury around me. I drifted off into a peaceful sleep. It felt good to be back in my own house again.

The baby was due within a month and Ma Costantino whipped the house into shape for me, typical of her style of doing things. The kids kept their things picked up, knowing she was right around the corner with a wooden spoon in her hand. She especially enjoyed working in the yard and kept all the kids busy doing little jobs. The place was immaculate.

I looked forward to Frank's Sunday furlough each week when we could spend some time together.

Debbie was born in December. Frank and I had started attending a local Episcopal church in St.

Cloud and I phoned the Priest, Fr. Harry Leventis, to make plans to have her baptized.

"I've been meaning to visit you and Frank," he said, "to talk about church membership, and the baby's baptism." He made an appointment for the next day. Membership was no problem, Frank was confirmed in the Catholic church and the Episcopal church would accept that. We set a tentative date for baptism. We had a friendly visit and on the way out he said, "By the way, we're having a special mid-week prayer service this week that you and Frank might be interested in." "I'm afraid Frank won't be able to come," I said, "because he only gets Sunday furloughs."

"Sunday furloughs?" he asked.

"Yes, Frank is still in prison." I explained to him that Frank was on work-release in Kissimmee. I could tell he was surprised and I wondered how he would handle it.

"Bunny, you and Frank are welcome in my church," he said. "Please come Sunday."

The following Sunday he spoke on God's forgiveness. "God is willing to forgive anyone," he began, "even a burglar or a murderer. But how would you people feel today if you had someone like that sitting next to you in the pew? Would you be able to accept him and forgive him as God does?"

He paused to let his point sink in. Then he invited Frank to come forward and share his conversion experience. It was very quiet and Frank had their full attention. He shared with them how God changed his life and gave him a new direction.

When He was through, Father Leventis welcomed us to the congregation and said he enjoyed Frank's occasional "Amen." "At least I knew somebody is listening and agreeing with what I'm saying," he said smilingly.

Many of the people came over to us on the way out, expressing their love and acceptance, and how much they enjoyed hearing Frank speak. We had found our church home.

December slipped by quickly and I was looking forward to spending the holidays as a family again. It had been so long; four years, but it seemed more like ten. Frank was given an overnight furlough and came home on Christmas Eve.

We didn't have much money to buy presents but we celebrated Christmas in a new spirit. Frank and I wrapped the gifts together on Christmas Eve after the kids were tucked in bed. We placed them under the Christmas tree and sat together in the quiet, enjoying a sense of Peace on Earth. The soft glow of the tree lights spilled through the room and the air smelled of pine. We sat talking until the early morning hours.

The kids came tumbling out of their beds early Christmas morning, eager to open the presents that had mysteriously appeared under the tree. A short time later there were torn wrapping papers and ribbons all over the room. Happy little faces were enjoying their new toys.

I helped Ma Costantino in the kitchen as we prepared some of Frank's favorite Italian dishes. He really enjoyed eating, but his stomach wasn't used to spicy food anymore, and he didn't keep it down for long. But he said it tasted so good it was worth it. It was a perfect day.

The following week he had another overnight furlough for New Years Eve. That had always been the hardest time for me while Frank was gone. I had felt terribly alone on those nights. But from now on, we'd start out each new year together.

I went to the Road Prison at 6 p.m. New Years Eve to pick him up. When I walked into the office, the Lieutenant said, "I'm sorry, Mrs. Costantino, but the Captain cancelled all furloughs today because the men came back drunk from their jobs."

I just stared at him, so he explained, "If he allows then to go out overnight, they'll probably get into trouble, with all the drinking that goes on for New Years Eve."

I couldn't hold back the tears. "I don't understand why Frank has to suffer because of the other men," I said. "Frank doesn't even drink. We were just planning to spend the evening at home."

I slumped into a chair and the Lieutenant said, "Let me make a phone call and see what I can do."

He called the Captain and explained that Frank had not come back drunk like the other guys and asked him to reconsider his furlough. He put down the receiver and smiled, "The Captain said Frank could go."

"Thank you," I said. "Thank you for caring."

"Frank's heard some good news today," the Lieutenant said, "but I'll let him tell you about it when he comes in." He grinned and I wondered what it was.

Frank came in a few minutes later and it was obvious he was excited.

"My release date has been set for January 11th."

Release? January 11th? Why, that's less than two weeks!

"Happy New Year!" the Lieutenant shouted as we headed out the door into the cold December air.

It truly would be a happy new year, I thought, as Frank and I walked arm in arm to the car.

As the January release date approached, there

was a little apprehension mixed in with the anticipation. We were getting along fine with Frank just being home on Sundays, but would that continue in the nitty gritty of everyday living? Would we be able to make the adjustments needed? What if his old friends looked him up? How would he handle that? How would the kids react to having him home all the time?

I baked a cake the day of his release and decorated it with "Welcome Home, Daddy." Frank decided to put in a full day's work on the construction job, because we needed the money. However, this time he was able to come home at 4:30 p.m. instead of going back to the Road Prison!

Frank's mother flew back to Boston now that Frank was home, and at first I found it difficult to adjust to the routine of having meals on time and getting the housework done with five kids. But it was so good to know that Frank would be home every night, and I enjoyed cooking for him. Anything I prepared was delicious to him after four years of prison food!

Every Friday night we would do the grocery shopping together and Frank handled all the finances. It felt so good to be taken care of again. He didn't go "Out" at all, and I soon relaxed, knowing that he had no intentions of going out and looking up his old friends.

The kids had a harder time adjusting to Frank being home than I did. Especially Lori, the oldest. Even though she was only nine years old, she was a little adult. I had leaned on her to help take care of the younger kids and help with the housework. She had been my companion and slept in the same bedroom. Now Frank was taking her place and she felt like she was being pushed out of my life. It was a confusing time for her and it took a while for her to be able to accept Frank in the role of her father again.

I was never strong on discipline, and without a man around to back me up, I had allowed the kids to become a bit unruly. Frank didn't want to have to spank them all the time and have them resent him for it. He had taken some psychology courses while in prison and decided to put it into practice with the kids.

Tony was seven years old and beginning to give me a hard time. Frank's advice was, "When Tony doesn't behave, just ignore him. Don't even talk to him. Then he'll feel like an outcast and start responding in order to be a part of the family again."

Our house was on Alligator Lake and I had made it very clear to the kids that they were not to go down by the water unsupervised. One day Tony decided to test me on that rule and casually strolled down to the water. I was watching him, but didn't stop him. Since I didn't yell at him, he continued on to the neighbor's boat dock and roamed out on it, peering out over the edge. He would glance my way every once in a while to see if I was still watching. I was relieved when he came back into the yard. He was surprised that I didn't do anything about it.

I just didn't talk to him the rest of the afternoon. It didn't take him long to figure out what was going on and I overheard him outside saying to Rocco, age five, "Hey, Rocco, come on, this is neat. Mom isn't going to talk to us anymore and we can do whatever we want."

They both headed down to the lake. I was fuming, but didn't say anything. Now I had two kids I couldn't speak to.

That night Tony refused to go to bed at the regular time, so we just ignored him. When we finally got ready for bed ourselves, Frank shut off the lights in the house, and Tony yelled, "Hey, who turned the lights off? I'm not going to bed."

We just let him sit there in the dark and went to bed ourselves.

The next morning I was about to cook some bacon and eggs, when Tony marched into the kitchen, picked up the bacon, threw it on the floor, and looked at me defiantly. I was so angry, I kicked him. But I didn't talk to him.

When Frank came home that night I said, "Frank, this psychology of yours is not working. I'm the one who has to put up with Tony's antics all day long, and I'm sick of it."

Frank called Tony into the room and said, "Pack your bags, Tony."

"Why, where are we going?" Tony asked.

"You're the one who's going." Frank said. "You don't respect your mother and you're not abiding by the rules, so you can just leave."

The calm intensity of Frank's voice had more impact on Tony than if Frank had yelled at him. Tony nervously glanced out the window and noticed that it was getting dark outside. His eyes grew large with fear.

"Come on," Frank said, "I'll help you pack."

He took Tony by the arm, marched him into the bedroom, and started putting his clothes into a paper bag. Tony started to cry. Frank kept packing. The crying turned to wailing.

Frank sat down next to him on the bed and said, "Listen, Tony, if you promise to start abiding by the rules of this house, you can stay. If not, you can leave. The choice is yours."

Tony agreed, between sobs, to be obedient and there was a big improvement in his behavior after that.

Frank soon discovered, however, that each of the

kids' personalities was very different and the method of discipline had to be adjusted accordingly. Michelle, for instance, would cry if she didn't get her own way. If I ignored her, she would simply cry for hours if necessary, and wear me down.

I remember the day we went shopping with all the kids for clothes. I had Debbie in the carriage and took Lori with me to one part of the store to buy a dress for her for school. Frank took Tony, Rocco, and Michelle to the snack bar and bought them a milk shake.

Michelle, who was four, kept swishing around on the stool. She thought it was neat that the seat turned all the way around and she kept spinning around and around.

"Cut that out," Frank said, "You're going to fall and knock over the milk shake."

She just ignored him and kept it up until she fell off the stool. Her arm hit the milk shake, which splattered all over Frank, Michelle and the floor. Frank began cleaning up the mess with napkins and said quietly, but intently, "Michelle, I'm going to kill you when we get out of here."

That's when I became aware of what was happening. From the other side of the store I could hear Michelle's screaming voice, "Pl – ee – ze don't kill me! Pl – ee – ze don't kill me!"

Frank whispered hoarsely, "Shut up!"

But she continued wailing at the top of her lungs, "Pl – ee – ze don't kill me! Pl – ee – ze don't beat me!"

It was quite a scene and Frank was totally embarrassed. I walked right past them and pretended I didn't know who they were.

When we got outside, Frank said to me, "Forget the psychology." Michelle got her first spanking.

Frank continued his job as a laborer for the Graves

Construction Company after he was released from prison. He worked hard and within a few months he was made foreman. From there he went to work for another company and continued moving up in position. When this company completed its work in our area, they were moving on to Fort Lauderdale to build a hospital there. They wanted Frank to come along and be their superintendent. But, after praying about it, we felt we weren't to move. We were finally getting settled and didn't want to uproot the kids again.

Another job opening came up after we decided to stay and Frank went to work as a general superintendent for Southeastern Walls and Ceilings, Inc. After about a year with them, he decided he knew enough about the business to step out on his own and opened up his own company, "Frank's Paint and Drywall."

Disneyworld had come into the area and the construction business was booming. Housing was needed for employees, and motels for the tourists. The combination of Frank's ability and the construction boom made the business an instant success.

Since the kids were getting more involved with school activities and Boy Scouts and Brownies, we decided to move closer to town. I was always driving one of the kids to a meeting and this would save on gas.

We contacted a realtor, but she said rentals were scarce and only knew of one place for rent. She asked for us, but when the owners heard about Frank's prison record, they refused to rent to us.

She called us back, suggesting we consider buying a house instead of renting.

"What do you have with a small down payment?" Frank asked.

"If you buy through F.H.A.," she said, "then you'd only need $1,000 down." She told us she was on the zoning board and would help in any way she could.

We discovered that F.H.A. required a two year emplyment record and Frank had only been out of prison for a year and a half at the time. We filled out the application anyway, and were honest about Frank's prison record.

Father Leventis, the rector of our church; Jimmy Chimento, a Christian who owned a local gas station, and Mel Wills, Frank's parole officer, all wrote letters of recommendation for us.

Six weeks later the loan went through. We knew God had His hand in it.

I called my sister Paula in Miami to share the good news about the house. She said she was happy for us, but I could tell by the tone of her voice that something was wrong.

"Mom isn't getting any better," she said. "I really think the Hodgkins Disease is beginning to take its toll on her."

I asked if she was well enough to come up for a visit with us and Paula said she was. So we made arrangements for her to fly to Orlando the following week.

Frank and I picked her up at the airport and when she came walking toward us I noticed she had that same gray look about her that my dad had before he died. She looked very tired.

Over the next few days she spent much of her time sleeping and began to complain of severe pain under her shoulder blades. I took her to a doctor and he felt it was arthritis that was giving her trouble, so he prescribed a pain reliever. But it didn't seem to help and she began to have trouble sleeping as the pain increased.

She had been very restless since my dad died and couldn't seem to find peace. She had done a lot of traveling back and forth to Massachusetts and admitted to me one day that no matter where she went, she felt lost and out of place.

I told her that Jesus could give her the peace she was looking for, as He had for me, but she got uncomfortable when I became so personal, and the conversation was awkward and stilted.

I wanted so much to throw my arms around her and tell her that I loved her and that God loved her, but I couldn't.

After several more days of increased pain we decided it would be best for her to fly back to Miami and check in with her own doctor there.

He put her into the hospital immediately. It was discovered that she had a swollen spleen. The Hodgkins Disease, a form of cancer, had already eaten away at her ribs. That was the reason for the increasing pain.

I wanted so badly to be with her, but it was a 220-mile drive and I didn't want to drive that distance alone with the kids. Frank's parole stipulation was that he couldn't enter Dade County, which is also where my mother was.

My brother Billy went to the State Attorney's Office, told them about my mother's condition, and explained Frank's situation. Billy asked that a letter be written to the Parole Board in Tallahassee, stating that Frank wouldn't be arrested if he entered Dade County. Then he went to the Mayor of Hialeah and made the same request.

Meanwhile, Frank's parole officer, Mel Wills,

also wrote to the Parole Board asking them to reconsider the Dade County restriction.

When Frank first came home from prison, Mel had said he didn't sleep all night after he had read Frank's criminal record. But he came to see that our lives really had changed and he became supportive of us.

Little did he know that his letter to the Parole Board was going to get him visits from the F.B.I. and other special law enforcement agencies. Frank was a major criminal and they spelled that out for him, but he remained firm in his belief that Frank had really changed.

The Parole Board granted the request on the condition that Frank call and check in with them as soon as he arrived at my mother's house. He had to remain at the house and call in again when leaving the area.

We abided by their request and made the weekend trip to Miami. While Frank stayed at the house with the kids, I spent my time at the hospital with my mother.

I helped feed and bathe her and fussed with her hair. I knew how much she loved blueberry cream cheese pie and brought her a piece the second day. She seemed to enjoy every bite I spoon-fed her.

When it was time for me to leave, she cried and wanted me to stay. We both sensed it would be the last time we would see each other. But I couldn't face talking about it and just said, "I'll see you next weekend."

I kissed her on her cheek and walked out of the room, knowing I would never see her alive again.

The following week Billy phoned and said, "Bunny, Mom's gone."

We had to go through the whole procedure with the Parole Board again in order to get permission to attend the funeral. The church service was to be held in Miami, but burial would take place in Massachusetts, as with my father.

I was told the casket would be closed and was relieved, but when we arrived at the funeral parlor, it was open. I forced myself to slowly walk over to the casket.

I stood in the silence of the chapel, staring down at her. Her dark hair was neatly brushed, her eyes closed as if sleeping, but it was like looking at a replica, an empty shell that once contained life. Now, there was nothing there.

I wanted to kiss her goodbye, but when my lips got as close as her hair, I just couldn't make contact. It was too late, she was gone. I wondered as I stood in the silence, staring down at her, did she ever really love me?

Finally, the lid of the coffin was brought down. It was over, but the tears would not come.

A week later I was having a restless night and tossed and turned trying to sleep. When I finally did fall asleep, I had a dream.

I seemed to be standing in outer space and it was dark all around me. I wasn't afraid of the dark and the stillness; I seemed to be waiting for something or someone. Then I noticed the shadow of a figure coming towards me and I strained my eyes, trying to see who it was. As the figure came closer, I recognized that it was my mother.

She stopped briefly in front of me, smiling, then reached out and hugged me, saying, "I love you, Bunny."

I woke up instantly, still feeling the touch of her arms around me. Tears of release came and the greyness that I had been feeling since the funeral began to dissolve, like the last spring snow melting in the warmth of the day.

I lay there a long time, allowing the tears to cleanse and bring healing. When they stopped, there was only the soft sound of the sleeping night. A deep peace came over me and covered me like a warm blanket as I closed my eyes and drifted into a restful sleep.

Chapter 12

"Who is Gordon Strongitharn?" I asked Frank as I was checking through the mail.

"He used to visit me in prison when I was at Belle Glade. You met Gordon and his wife, Bernice, at Dunklin Memorial Camp."

I couldn't remember meeting them. "What's he doing in South America?" I asked as I checked the postmark on the envelope.

"They're working there as missionaries and live on a houseboat on the Amazon River," Frank said. I shuddered as I imagined the snakes, spiders and other creatures they must have to put up with.

"What would you think about us doing something like that?" Frank asked.

"Oh my god, Frank!" Then I noticed he was standing there grinning at me. I breathed a sign of relief. He wasn't serious.

After he read Gordon's letter, Frank asked me to answer it. "After working twelve hours a day, I don't particularly feel like writing letters at night," he said.

I agreed, and I developed a friendship with the Strongitharns through the mail. Although we were attending church regularly, I hadn't developed any close Christian friendships and the letters from Gordon and Bernice provided some of the fellowship

I needed. I asked them many of the questions I still had about the Christian walk, and eagerly waited for their replies. The letters were almost like a Bible correspondence course for me and were the source of my spiritual growth for about a year.

Chaplain Max Jones also had kept in touch with us since Frank's release. He had been transferred from Belle Glade and was now serving as chaplain at Florida State Prison. He called one day and asked Frank to drive up on Sunday and speak for the chapel service. He felt that because Frank had served two years of his time at Raiford, the inmates would be able to relate to him.

Frank struggled with his answer. He felt it would be difficult to go back to Raiford and walk behind those prison walls. There were so many bad memories. I wasn't very enthusiastic about it either, because Sunday was his only day off and he worked so hard during the week. But, after praying about it, we both felt he should go. We knew it would mean a lot to the inmates to have him come back and talk to them.

The first Sunday he came back looking dejected and I was almost afraid to ask him how it went.

"The guard in the tower gave me some lip and it brought back all that hate and resentment," he said. "Then I had to go into the chapel and be a blessing to everyone."

But he continued to go and each time things got better. One particular Sunday there were three guards in the service and by the time it was over, all three of them were reduced to tears, as they listened to how God had changed the direction of Frank's life. Several of the guards turned their lives over to Christ as a result of those services. They believed if God could change Frank's life, then He could certainly help them, too.

It was quite an experience for Frank to kneel at the altar and pray with a guard, – someone he once hated, but now knew Jesus loved, and he could love, too. Only God can make enemies brothers. It was the beginning of an inner healing process.

That healing and growth continued through a "Faith Alive" weekend announced at our church one Sunday. It was to be a first for our church and the purpose was for personal spiritual growth and learning how to share your faith with others. Frank thought it would be good for us to go. We needed to become involved with other active laymen. Some people called it the Charismatic renewal, but I didn't quite know what that meant.

I did like the people involved, and I could see very clearly they loved the Lord. In spite of that, I was still a bit apprehensive about it, but we signed up and I began looking forward to meeting Christians from other churches who would be there.

The first session started like any general sharing meeting with some of the team sharing testimonies. After the general sharing time, we broke into small groups.

At the close of the group session, the team leader suggested we have a prayer time together. I tensed up as I realized everyone was taking a turn praying out loud in front of others. I always left that up to Frank.

When my turn came, I nervously prayed, "Thank you, Jesus, for my family." I immediately felt better for doing it.

The fact that I was so nervous made me realize how much growing I had to do yet, but I wanted to grow.

I threw myself into the rest of the weekend, soaking up everything God had to give me.

After a few days, Fr. Leventis called a group of us together to evaluate the effect of the weekend.

"What effect did it have on you personally?" he asked.

I was the first one to respond, speaking with new-found boldness.

All agreed the weekend was a spiritual highlight in our little church, and I felt like I belonged.

After the meeting Fr. Leventis asked Frank and me if we would like to sign up to be team members on a Faith Alive weekend going into another church.

I was so high spiritually that I said yes without considering what was expected of me.

The weekend was to be in a church in Ft. Lauderdale, Florida, and as the weekend drew near, so did the sense of anticipation. It was to be my first time going out to minister for God.

The trip down to Ft. Lauderdale flew past, and we were soon saying hello to the couple we were to spend the weekend with.

All the team members were meeting in the church for the planning sessions that preceded the weekend.

One of the requirements for a team member was to share a personal testimony of meeting Jesus Christ. I was terrified as the various meetings were assigned, and half hoping they would have more people to speak than spots to speak in.

My thoughts flashed back to the blessings I had received at Faith Alive at our church and a new sense of determination started to flow through me. I knew I couldn't back down, no matter how nervous I was. I had made a commitment and had to stick to it.

I chose to share at a Women's Luncheon at the church and somehow got through it, even though my whole body was trembling with fear, and my voice sounded abnormal.

Mary Canada, whom I had met at the Faith Alive weekend, came up to me afterwards and said, "Bunny, that was great!"

Another woman said, "Your eyes just sparkled as you shared."

I was so nervous, I couldn't even remember what I had said. I was so relieved it was over, but glad that I had stuck to my commitment.

Chapter 13

Mary Canada and I became great friends after the weekend. Frank used to say, "Any time Bunny wants to know what God is saying to her she calls Mary."

Both she and Dick, her husband, were to become our lifelong friends.

A whole new horizon of Christian life and living was opening up to me. I had friends, and they didn't look at me like a second hand citizen of the Kingdom. To them Frank's past was secondary to the miracle of salvation God had worked in his life. I wanted to meet more of God's wonderful family.

Mary told me about the women's prayer groups that were held in homes in our area and I started going twice a week. I was like a dry sponge, soaking up everything I could. I felt like I had so much to learn and to experience, and I wanted it all!

The meetings included singing, sharing, praying for one another, and a Bible lesson. I loved it and gradually got up the courage to participate instead of just observing.

Some of the women were more enthusiastic than others. At first I thought it was just a difference in their personalities, but I gradually realized it went beyond their natural make-up. These were the ones who had received what they called the Baptism of the

Holy Spirit. I had never heard of that term before. I just knew they had a dimension to their spiritual lives that I lacked. I began to seek God for the Baptism of the Holy Spirit.

A few months later, Gordon and Bernice Strong-itharn called. They were back from South America and wanted us to come visit them in Melbourne, Florida. They invited us down on a Sunday so that we could attend services at The Tabernacle with them.

We were familiar with Jamie Buckingham, pastor of The Tabernacle. Several of the books he had written were being passed around our prayer group. We had talked about inviting him to our area as a guest speaker, so we called several friends and invited them to come and hear Jamie preach.

We arrived just after the service had begun and we walked into an atmosphere of praise and worship. The people were happy and everyone was clapping hands to the beat of the music. I recognized that many of the songs were Scripture verses put to music. Gradually the tempo of the songs slowed into a quiet, worshipful mood. People's eyes were closed, faces uplifted and hands raised. It was the most beautiful singing I had ever heard.

Then, as if some unseen choir director had given a signal, they began singing a new song. The harmony was beautiful. After a few minutes I realized they were singing in the Spirit. Some were singing in tongues, some in English, but it all blended perfectly. The music rose and fell in perfect timing as they sang, most with eyes closed.

I felt I was standing on holy ground as I listened to these beautiful praises ascending to God. Then, suddenly, the music stopped. It was very quiet and no one moved.

Jamie broke the silence. "Somebody here has been seeking the Baptism of the Holy Spirit. If she will just stand up now, she'll receive what she desires from God."

"That must be what they call a Word of Knowledge," I thought. We had read about the gifts of the Spirit in I Corinthians 12 in our prayer group, but I had never seen them in operation, like this, before. I looked around and waited for someone to stand up. No one did.

He repeated it a second time. "Somebody here has been seeking the Baptism of the Holy Spirit. If she'll stand now, she'll receive from God."

I suddenly realized he was talking about me. How could he know? My heart started pounding. I didn't want to stand up in front of all these people. I didn't know what would happen if I received the Baptism of the Holy Spirit. What if I started speaking in tongues or something? I would be so embarrassed.

He repeated it a third time. No one stirred. I was sure the people around me could hear my heart pounding. Finally he said, "Okay, sit there and be miserable," and he went on with the service.

On the way home, everyone in the car was bubbling over with excitement about how great the service was, but I was miserable. My self-consciousness had robbed me of an opportunity to receive a special blessing from God. I had trouble getting to sleep that night.

The next morning at the women's prayer meeting, I told them what had happened and asked them to pray for me. I was assured by one of the women that God would not force me to speak in tongues, or do anything else that would be embarrassing to me. He simply wanted to reveal more of Himself to me and provide the power for overcoming problems through His Spirit.

I realized that the problem I had been having was one of trust. I had never totally trusted anyone in my entire life, and now God was asking that of me.

He wanted me to have a complete trust in Him. I believed in Him, knew He loved me, but had never taken that step of complete abandonment of my life to Him. This was another step of faith.

Marcia Loeffler, one of the women in the prayer group, said to me, "You may not feel any different when we pray for you. Not everyone has an emotional experience. In faith just believe that God is giving you what you've asked for. As you confess it and share it with others, the feelings will follow."

Then several of the women laid hands on me and prayed for me to be filled with the Spirit. I simply prayed, "Lord, unto You do I commend my spirit."

When I got home from the prayer meeting, I phoned my friend Mary Canada and told her what had happened. As I talked to her, I could feel a new joy bubbling up inside. She was happy for me. Then I phoned another friend, and the joy increased. By the time Frank came home that night, I felt like I was on cloud nine.

I couldn't wait until Thursday night of that week. Jamie Buckingham had agreed to come up and talk to our prayer group, including the men. We thought it would be good if we could start meeting as couples, rather than just the women meeting separately. The men agreed and 40 people showed up.

When Jamie arrived, I immediately told him what had happened to me in his service and how I had received the Baptism of the Holy Spirit the next day. He smiled and said, "I knew it was you."

He then spoke to the group, sharing the principles

of how to have a good couple's prayer group and a Bible study. Afterwards he offered to pray for anyone with needs. Dr. Cal McGoogan, a local optometrist, was there with his wife, Gail. Cal had been in traction and was having a lot of back pain. Dick Loeffler, a chiropractor who had been treating Cal, was there also. Dick's wife, Marcia, and Cal's wife, Gail, were members of the prayer group that had prayed for me for the Baptism of the Holy Spirit.

Dick was very skeptical about praying for healing and just sat back and observed. When Jamie prayed for Cal, the pain left instantly. Then he prayed for Cal to receive the Baptism of the Holy Spirit.

One by one different people were prayed for and needs were met. Dick Loeffler was amazed at Cal's response to prayer, but still skeptical about whether a healing had actually taken place. Over the next weeks he observed him both as a friend and a patient, and the healing was confirmed. That opened up a whole new understanding of the power of prayer for Dick, as well as for Cal and the rest of us.

Gordon and Bernice Strongitharn drove up from Melbourne to lead the Bible study. Every time we met I would wonder, "What's going to happen tonight? What's happened in the lives of our friends this week?" Others were being touched by our lives.

I remember the night when a young woman came to our door selling vacuum cleaners. It was just before Frank came home, and she aggressively set up her display in our living room.

Frank came in shortly afterwards, looked at all the stuff strewn around and said, "What's going on here, Bunny?"

"This is Scottie," I said. "She's selling vacuum cleaners."

"We don't need a vacuum cleaner, Bunny."

"Most people think that way," Scottie chimed in, "until they see the features of this vacuum."

Frank remained firm and said, "We don't need a vacuum cleaner. Please put your stuff away."

"You don't like people, do you?" Scottie said.

"I like people," Frank told her. "I just don't want your vacuum cleaner. In fact, I'm getting ready to have some coffee, and if you'll put your vacuum away, I'll make you a cup, too."

Frank served the coffee while Scottie and I talked. She was very bubbly and laughed a lot. The tempo of the conversation changed and Frank asked her what was the horrible pain that was inside her.

"What pain? What are you talking about?" she said.

"God is showing me that your heart is breaking," Frank told her. "The only reason He's showing me that is so He can minister to you. He loves you, Scottie."

She started crying. The tears rolled down her cheeks. "I thought I had that well hidden," she said.

She told us her story. It was less than a month before Christmas and her husband had taken their two-year-old child and left with another woman. She didn't know where he and the child were, the only employment she could find was selling vacuum cleaners door-to-door.

"God wants to come into your life and help you put it back together."

She looked at me and asked, "How can he know what's going on inside of me? I don't believe this is happening."

I assured her that God loved her and shared part of my story with her. Then we invited her to ask Jesus into her heart.

As the tears flowed, I knew that God was relieving her of the pain in her heart. She was a different woman when she left our house that night.

Frank began going into the prisons more often to minister and he took some of the men from the prayer group with him. A revival began in Florida State Prison during this time under the ministry of Chaplain Max Jones. When the prison rules were changed to allow women to come to the chapel services, we went as couples.

The inmates were always enthusiastic and we just loved them. They were so hungry for God and His Word. We would have to get up at 3 a.m. in order to get there on time for the services. (It was a four-hour drive.) Some of the inmates got up even earlier to pray for us during our traveling time and to pray for the services.

When Christmas arrived, we wanted to make it a special time for the inmates, knowing what it's like to be separated from your family during the holidays. Our prayer group brought them gifts, made bookmarks for their Bibles, crosses for them to wear, brought instruments for the Christian band they were forming, home-baked goods, a birthday cake for Jesus, and to top it off, about 300 meatballs requested by one of Frank's old friends!

We all agreed that it was one of the best Christmas celebrations we ever had. There was such love and compassion flowing, and our hearts overflowed towards God.

There are so many special memories of those visits – the inmate band playing for us; Jack Murphy playing the Lord's Prayer on his violin; the Christmas pageant the inmates wrote and performed; the times we stopped at 4 a.m. and bought 15 dozen doughnuts to bring to the inmates; the inmate who cried because he hadn't eaten a blueberry doughnut in 17 years, and the inmate who got his license to preach and was baptizing men in the toilet!

And then there was Pops. He woke up from a sound sleep in his cell one night, feeling an urgency to pray for Frank. As he prayed, he felt that something was wrong, so he woke up several other inmates to pray along with him.

In the morning Chaplain Jones told them that Frank's mother had a heart attack during the night and Frank was flying to Boston to see her. They were so excited that God woke them up to pray when they didn't even know what was going on. They began praying for healing for Frank's mother and she had a quick recovery. Frank also had the opportunity to pray with his mother to be healed.

Later, we shared with Ma Costantino how the men at Raiford had been faithfully praying for her. She was really touched. On one of her trips to visit us, she went with us to Raiford to meet Pops and thank him for his prayers. They wept in each other's arms.

The word started spreading around town. People were talking about our lives and ministry. The nurse at the local health center referred a woman to us for prayer because her baby had been sent home to her to die. The doctors had given the baby a few weeks to live. All of her internal organs were mis-located. We prayed, and now, seven years later, the mother calls her daughter a miracle baby.

There was another woman in her seventies who had terminal Parkinson's Disease. She approached Frank in a restaurant where he was having coffee and asked, "Are you a priest?"

"No," he said, sensing that something was wrong. "Why do you ask?"

"I'm going to commit suicide," the old lady told

him. "I'm going to die soon anyhow. I have Parkinson's Disease and I don't want to be a burden to my family."

Frank asked her to sit down and he called Dr. Dick Loeffler. "Dick, there's an old lady over here who is suicidal. Can you pray with me for her?"

They went to Dick's office and prayed. She was healed, told all her friends, and joined our prayer group!

Poor Dick! This was almost too much for his scientific mind. He told Frank when the woman left his office, "This is medically impossible."

The requests began pouring in for Frank to go and speak and teach, in the prisons, in home prayer groups, and in churches. He could hardly keep up with it all. I took on the responsibility of answering the inmate mail that arrived daily and was steadily increasing.

Then, in the middle of all this activity, the construction boom came to a standstill. Gas rationing was put into effect and things were tight for everyone. Frank decided to close his company before the bottom fell out, and get a regular job. That would also free him up for more time in the ministry. Although he was willing to work at anything, he just couldn't come up with another job.

I was talking to Marcia Loeffler one day and said, "I don't understand what God is trying to tell us. No matter how hard Frank tries, he can't find a job."

"You know, Bunny," she said, "God might be telling you and Frank that it's time to go into a faith ministry. I don't know if I could do something like that, and I only have two children, while you have five. But I believe that is what God is calling you to."

"You've got to be kidding!" I said. "A faith ministry? Waiting for people to send us money in dribbles and drabbles to live on? I could never live like that."

But even while the words spilled out of me, deep inside there was a still small voice that said she was right.

When I mentioned the conversation to Frank, he said, "She's right. I have felt God telling me the same thing."

"But where will the money come from?" I protested.

"If God wants me to be His employee, He will pay me, just like I paid my own employees in my company."

It was obvious that he had thought it through and it was already settled in his mind and heart.

We had to begin living one day at a time and my trust was put to the test. Each day I anxiously opened the mail, hoping there would be some donations contained in the letters. If there was $10, I took it and bought groceries for the day. But there never was enough to cover the other household expenses and before long we were three months behind on our house payments, as well as other bills.

That's when one of Frank's old buddies showed up. He found out about our situation and said, "Come on, Frank, let's just go out together one night, for old times sake. Man, in one haul, we could easily "make" enough money for you to pay off all your debts and still have some left over."

"No thanks, pal," Frank said. "Somehow God will provide for our needs."

"Man, you're crazy," he said as he left.

I really thought things would improve after that test, and the money would come pouring in. After all, doesn't God bless His children when they're obedient? But things got worse.

I became angry with God. It seemed to me He wasn't being very faithful to us. I went into the bedroom one afternoon and got down on my knees.

"I just don't understand you, God. I've tried to praise You through all of this, but it's getting harder. I'm not asking for luxuries, just for food and necessities. I know this isn't Frank's fault. He's serving You and doing the best he can. Your Word teaches us to pay our debts and not owe people money. But if You don't provide for us, how can we do this?"

"I don't even know how to approach You any more. Praising hasn't worked. Asking hasn't worked. I feel like You're up there watching and listening, but doing nothing. You're going to have to tell me what You expect of me, because I'm confused. Right now I really don't feel like ever getting down on my knees again to even talk to You."

I just sat there in the silence for a while. Then, from somewhere deep within my soul, I heard, "My ways are not your ways and my thoughts are not your thoughts. You are rebelling against my ways because you have limited understanding. But it's okay, and I want you to know that I love you. Your needs will be met. Just continue to trust."

I wept as I experienced wave after wave of God's love. It was as if I was bathed in liquid love. I got up off my knees with renewed trust.

The phone was jangling off the hook. I hurried to the kitchen to answer it. "Hi, Bunny, this is Ben Harrison. I just phoned to tell you that God has impressed upon me that I should help you and Frank out. I've got $1,000 to help you catch up on your back house payments." I was barely able to choke out a thank-you.

Later Dick Loeffler called saying he wanted to give us monthly support. Kirk Bock stopped by, saying he noticed that our car was falling apart and he wanted to buy us another one.

Then there was the night at supper time when I said to Frank, "We don't have anything to eat tonight. We're even out of bread." "We've got to trust God, Bunny," Frank said as he put his arm around me. "He'll provide."

I set the table and we blessed the empty plates. About 30 minutes later, there was a knock at the door. It was Don Brown, a member of our prayer group.

"I just picked up all the meat from a cow that I had slaughtered. It's all packaged for my freezer, but Diane and I would like to share half of it with you, if that's okay."

From an empty table to a steak dinner, with plenty for many meals to come! Whether it's five, or five thousand, God provides for His children, with twelve basketsful left over!

There were so many other times that God provided through our friends and prayer group members. Dan and Terry Horton would show up periodically with bags of groceries, always just when we needed them most. The prayer groups where Frank taught took up collections for us. Bit by bit the money was there as we needed it.

During this time I became pregnant with our sixth child and it concerned me that we would have another mouth to feed. But God was faithful. There were six baby showers given for me and I had more than I needed. We named the baby Maranatha, meaning "The Lord has come."

At this time my brother Billy, who had become a Christian, wrote a letter to Pat Robertson of the "700

Club" telling him about Frank's conversion and ministry. Pat contacted Frank and invited him to be a guest on one of his television programs, a Christian talk show. Pat was impressed with what God was doing in Frank's life and began to help support his ministry.

Frank incorporated Christian Prison Ministries and many of the men from the prayer group formed his board of directors. They said their main job was to keep Frank earthbound, because he had so many dreams and ideas!

He followed through with one of his dreams and opened Genesis II, a Christian supper club in Orlando. There was good Italian food as well as gospel singing and entertainment each night. Many lives were touched and changed as a result of it. The board of directors decided to close it in less than a year, because of the financial risk and other obligations, but there was much spiritual fruit produced from it, even in that time.

Then Pat Robertson asked Frank to take over the Video Discipleship Program that was in 80 prisons, as well as their outreach into the prisons. Chaplain Ray Hoekstra of International Prison Ministry asked Frank to write his autobiography as an outreach to inmates, and *Holes In Time* was published.

He appeared on Jim Bakker's PTL Club. He began lecturing in colleges and universities on the criminal justice system. He received an appointment from the Governor of Florida to serve as a member on the Region III Advisory Council for the Department of Corrections. He began working toward his dream of building an After Care center for released inmates.

I could hardly keep up with the rapid growth of the ministry. It overwhelmed me. I was proud of Frank and his abilities, and yet I recognized that only God could bring this about, all that was happening to us.

"How would you like to be married to an ordained man?" It was Frank just returning from a visit with Bishop William Folwell.

He was the Episcopal Bishop covering the churches in central Florida. He was interested in Frank's prison ministry and offered the cooperation and finanicial support of the church.

"What are you talking about?" I asked.

"The Bishop thinks I ought to attend the Institute for Christian Studies and become ordained. That would give me the covering of the church on my ministry and it would be of benefit in hearing the confession of the inmates."

I didn't respond, so he continued, "The Bishop will even pay the cost of the schooling through scholarships."

I could tell by the tone of his voice that he had already made up his mind.

I didn't want to be the wife of a clergyman. Even though Frank was already in ministry I felt being officially tagged as clergy would place new demands on me. We would live in a glass house and everyone would expect me to be a perfect example. How could I ever live up to an image like that?

Frank went ahead with the schooling and then plans were made for the ordination. During this whole time I was struggling with my own feelings of inadequacy in being put in the classification of clergyman's wife.

The week before the ordination I went on a Cursillo weekend. It was a personal spiritual retreat of renewal sponsored by the Episcopal church.

During one of the quiet times, I noticed a priest sitting down by the edge of the water reading his

Bible. I wandered over to him and began sharing what I was going through concerning Frank's upcoming ordination.

He had been reading Psalm 40 and shared it with me: *"I waited patiently for the Lord; and he inclined unto me, and heard my cry. He brought me up also out of a horrible pit, out of the miry clay, set my feet upon a rock, and established my going. And He put a new song in my mouth, even praise unto God: many shall see it, and fear, and shall trust in the Lord . . . Blessed is that man that maketh the Lord his trust . . . Many, O Lord my God, are thy wonderful works which thou hast done . . . . if I would declare and speak of them, they are more than can be numbered . . . "*

I went into the chapel to meditate and pray. God certainly had brought me out of the horrible pit of my former life. And he set my feet upon Jesus, the rock. He put a new song in my heart and did many miracles in my life. I certainly *had* discovered I could trust Him . . . If Frank's ordination would further God's purpose in our lives, then I should be willing to trust Him to help me with my part in it . . . *"Not my will, but thine be done,"* I prayed. I felt released and complete peace enveloped me.

June 23, 1979, five years after we had stepped out into a faith ministry, the day of Frank's ordination arrived. Everyone stood and St. Luke's Cathedral in Orlando reverberated with the sound of majestic music as the Bishop, priests, and the Avon Park inmate choir came in procession down to the altar.

Bishop Folwell's voice echoed, "Bless the Lord who forgives all our sins."

The people responded, "His mercy endures forever."

Everyone was seated while Father Leventis and

Chaplain Max Jones, the man who had led Frank to the Lord, presented Frank before the Bishop.

The Bishop then motioned for the audience to rise again as he said, "Dear friends in Christ, you know the importance of this ministry, and the weight of your responsibility in presenting Frank Costantino for ordination to the sacred order of Deacons. Therefore, if any of you know any impediment or crime because of which we should not proceed, come forward now and make it known." *"Any impediment or crime."* The words reverberated through my mind as the Bishop's words echoed through the Cathedral. Tears of gratitude splashed down my cheeks as I thought of God's total forgiveness.

We were seated as Father Al Durrance gave the sermon and the congregation recited the Nicene Creed. Bishop Folwell then stood up and laid hands on Frank as he said the prayer of consecration. Father Leventis ceremoniously placed the red stole vestment across Frank's white robe.

The Bishop then handed Frank a Bible as he said with his full, rich voice, "Receive this Bible as the sign of your authority to proclaim God's Word and to assist in the ministration of His Holy Sacraments."

Communion was prepared and the congregation was invited forward to receive. As I held out my hands to receive the Body of Christ, it was Frank who served me. Communion took on a new meaning for me that day.

At the close of the service, Frank's authoritative voice resounded through the Cathedral, "Let us go forth into the world, rejoicing in the power of the Spirit."

Chapter 14

"What is your ministry?" I thought as I licked the stamps and pressed them on the envelopes. All of today's letters were going to inmates at Raiford State Prison. As I sealed the last one, I prayed, "God, let these bring encouragement and offer the hope that is so badly needed in their lives."

As I placed them in our mailbox, the mailman arrived with a new batch that would need answering. It was difficult to keep up with all of it. The first one I opened was from an inmate who was doing time for murder.

He wrote, "Just as the safecracker's fingers need sensitizing to the safe's tumblers, so does the soul need spiritual sensitizing to Christ's word. Be assured that your letters to me have served, not only as a spiritual sensitizer, but as a tonic for my oft-sagging spirits."

The phone interrupted my reading. It was Chaplain Preston from the Florida Correctional Institute for Women in Lowell.

"Bunny, would you be willing to come to Lowell and minister to the women here one day a week?"

He knew of Frank's ministry and thought I would be able to relate to the women.

"These girls really have poor self-images and none

of the prison programs deal with that. Your life and what you have been through could give them hope."

I hesitated, wondering if I could really be of much help. This would be a big step, going out to minister on my own. Then I remembered Jesus' words . . . "I was in prison and you visited me . . . " I put aside my reservations and agreed to go up the following Saturday. Chaplain Preston was elated.

That Saturday 40 women came down to the chapel. I decided to have them watch a Bible teaching on closed circuit T.V. and we could discuss it afterwards.

"If anyone feels the need of some personal counseling," I said, "I'd be happy to talk with you alone while the others are watching television."

As everyone settled down to watch the program, I noticed that one of the women seemed very restless. After several minutes of fidgeting and shifting around in her chair she came over to me and asked if we could talk in private.

I took her into the Chaplain's office. He was gone for the day and I knew we could have privacy there.

As I closed the door, she began to cry.

"What's wrong?" I asked gently.

"I don't know," she said as she slumped into a chair. "I should be happy. I'm getting out in a couple of weeks and going home to my children."

"Are you afraid you won't be able to make it on the outside?" I asked.

She nodded as tears continued. "I've become a Christian while in here, but what will happen if I slip up? What if I'm not strong enough to make it out there? If I don't make it this time, then there's no hope left for me."

"Your commitment to Christ is real," I said, "And

you're a new creature in Christ according to the Bible. Old things have passed away and all things have become new. I read II Corinthians 5:17 to her and told her about how Jesus had changed my life and through Him I was overcoming my problems.

"In Hebrews 13:5 it says that God will never leave you or forsake you," I said. "As you step out beyond these prison walls, God will go with you. Your part is to trust Him to lead you and to keep you."

We prayed together and the peace of God replaced the tension she had been feeling.

The program was ending as we stepped back into the chapel and everyone broke for lunch, returning at one o'clock for a discussion time.

First, we sang some choruses, then we talked about the problems and fears they were facing in prison, and their concerns about families and loved ones. We applied the Scriptures to the problems and prayed for one another, encouraging and building each other up.

In the year that followed, I learned to trust God to give me the words I needed as I ministered to the women at Lowell. I felt as though my life had certainly been enriched, – a very great deal more than had theirs.

One Sunday my girlfriend Betty stopped by to visit me. I shared with her about my ministry to the women inmates.

"You have a lot more to offer people than you realize, Bunny," she said. "You have many abilities you haven't tapped yet."

"You're right, Betty. There is one thing I've always wanted to do, but it seems so far-fetched."

"What?" she asked curiously.

"Well, I've always had this secret desire to be a nurse. But I don't even have a high school diploma."

Betty worked for the CETA program and suggested I check into enrolling in school through them.

"With Frank's income, I'm sure you'd qualify," she said.

"You mean they would pay for the training?" I asked.

She nodded. "Why don't you go down and take the high school equivalency GED test. The next one is being given in two weeks. If you pass that, you'll qualify for the nursing course."

"Two weeks? But I've been out of school for 17 years! How can I study and be ready to take that test in two weeks?"

"You can do it, Bunny," Frank said as he came into the room. "Why not give it a try?"

The next day I went to the library, checked out the appropriate books and studied five hours a day for the next two weeks.

I was extremely nervous the day of the test, but was able to answer all the questions. The results didn't arrive in the mail until four weeks later. I was afraid to open the envelope. What if I failed? Even if I failed in only one section, I still wouldn't get my diploma.

My hands were shaking as I slowly opened it. As I unfolded the paper inside, I realized it was my diploma. I sat there holding it, running my fingers over the large letters that spelled my name, and cried.

The next day I enrolled in nursing school. I passed the physical, along with the entry exam, and was accepted as a student. CETA agreed to pay for babysitting, uniform, and books. I was overjoyed.

The first day of school I felt like a little kid starting

kindergarten. Excited, but afraid. I wasn't sure I could handle it. As I sat in my first class I thought, what am I doing here? This surely isn't me. I belong home changing diapers.

There was so much material to grasp! I wondered if I could absorb it all. Finally, two o'clock arrived. The homework assignments were given and I headed for home.

I was up most of the night studying. I had trouble understanding it all and I began to feel I was in over my head. I was exhausted the next morning, but made it to school on time for the 7:30 a.m. class.

I didn't have all the assignments completed and I was very frustrated. Then I discovered that I was supposed to take all week to complete them, not do them in one night. What a relief! I had really begun to think I had bitten off more than I could chew.

During my second week of school Frank was up in New England, speaking in some of the prisons and churches there. I began having trouble coping with my schedule, the housework, homework, the kids. There were just too many demands on my time. I yelled at the kids, "Everybody wants a piece of the rock, and I don't have it to give." They backed off and I cried in frustration.

Frank called me from Massachusetts and asked, "Is there something wrong at home? I felt the Lord telling me to call you."

I burst into tears and said, "Frank, I can't seem to get things together. Maybe I shouldn't be going to school."

"You can do it, I know you can," he said. "Look, I'll cancel the rest of my trip here, and catch the next flight home. You just hang in there."

Once he came home, everything seemed to fall into place. I just needed his help and support.

After completing the first four months of class-room work, we started going into the hospital two days per week. I enjoyed the patient contact, but also felt the tremendous responsibility of having people's lives in my hands. It made me work hard at learning all that I could.

It seemed so strange bringing home a report card to Frank and the kids. Lori signed the first one on the back and wrote in the remarks section:

> Mrs. O'Brien,
>
> I would like to arrange a child-teacher conference about my mother's grades.
> Also, if my mother acts up in class or tries to be the class clown, please let me know by sending home a note. – – (Pin it to her blouse.)
>
> Lori Costantino

When my year of school was almost over, it was time for me to order graduation invitations. I was planning to order about 100, but waited to see what the other students ordered. Some ordered five; the most one ordered was twenty. I cut my order down to 75. I was teased constantly after that.

"Bunny's inviting everyone she knows. The auditorium won't be big enough!"

One morning when I was working at the hospital, Mrs. Newman, one of my teachers, asked, "Do you belong to the LPN Association, Cheryl?" She always called me Cheryl, instead of Bunny like everyone else.

"Yes, I do," I said.

"Well, she said casually, "we had a staff meeting yesterday and we would like to nominate you as the representative of our school for the LPN of the Year Award. Would you accept the nomination?"

I just stared at her in disbelief, so she continued, "We need to know your answer so that we can complete the paperwork and send it in on time."

Why me? I wondered. There were other students who made better grades. I heard that our school hadn't had anyone win that award for 20 years. In fact, they hadn't even bothered to send a nominee for the past three years.

She stood there waiting for my answer. I managed to get out a "Yes, I guess that would be okay."

When I was leaving the hospital that afternoon one of the students came running over to me. "Oh, Bunny, I just heard the good news. That's such an honor. I'm so happy for you."

"I, I don't want to talk about it right now," I said. "I've always been such a loser. I'm having trouble dealing with this." I headed for the car and drove home in a daze.

When I walked into the house, I burst into tears. Lori came over to me and asked, "What's wrong? Did one of your patients die?"

I shook my head no.

"Did you get kicked out of school?"

"No," I cried, "I was just nominated for LPN of the Year for the state of Florida."

"And you're crying over that?" she asked.

"You don't understand," I said. "I don't feel like I deserve this."

By the next day, everyone at school heard about it and the place was buzzing. "Do you think our school finally has a chance to win?"

"You've got to do it for us, Bunny."

"Nobody's won in 20 years from our school, but you can do it."

I began to wish they had picked someone else. I hated the thought of letting them all down.

I had to fill out a report on my background for the nomination papers. They wanted to know about my achievements and community involvement, things like that. I couldn't think of much to write. I really wasn't into community involvement, and I certainly didn't consider myself an achiever, so I wrote about my prison ministry in Lowell and Raiford and turned it in.

A few days later I received a phone call from Rev. Huey Perry. He was the Associate Director of the Chaplaincy Division for the Home Mission Board of the Southern Baptist Convention. He knew Frank and me because of the impact of our ministry to inmates in the Florida correctional system.

He asked if I would consider speaking at a workshop on inmate families at the Congress of Corrections in San Diego.

"We'd like you to share what it felt like to be the wife of a convicted felon and share some of the experiences you went through while Frank was in prison. The audience will all be people connected with the criminal justice system – judges, lawyers, parole officers, policemen, social workers, etc. You and Frank have been through the entire experience of crime, prison, and rehabilitation. You were able to make the adjustments that kept your family together. The criminal justice people need to hear what you consider to be the reason for your success."

"I don't know," I said. "Although being the wife of a convicted felon means I can understand what the inmate family goes through, it doesn't make me a public speaker."

"I'm sure you'll do just fine. Just share from your heart."

I said I would go, but after I hung up I had second thoughts. It bugged me that the criminal justice people seemed to think that Frank was the only one who had to serve his sentence. I wondered how many of them realized when a judge sends a man to prison, he sentences that man's family as well.

I knew I had some things to say, but did I want to bare my soul in front of that many people? Will they really care about how I feel? Or are they just looking for a speaker to fill a spot in their program?

I was surprised at the intense feelings which were coming out of me. It made me realize that I hadn't totally dealt with the emotions and trauma of the past years. There were still some suppressed areas of hurt and anger buried within me. How could I share with others a way to cope if I lacked a complete emotional healing myself?

I discussed it with Frank and he suggested that I talk with Father Al Durrance who had a ministry of inner healing and healing of memories. Al was Frank's spiritual director and one of the earliest supporters of our ministry. "He's the best I know, Bunny."

I went to him and we went through my childhood years, adolescence, and all the other stages of my life. We talked through specific incidents that came to my mind and then dealt with the emotions that surfaced along with each of the memories.

The most difficult thing I had to deal with was forgiveness, not of others, but of myself. I wasn't able to forgive myself for not being stronger and more able to cope during those years that Frank was in prison.

After the first session I was depressed for two days. A lot of stuff that had been buried in my subconscious was beginning to surface. Father Durrance explained to me that God wanted to take each of those hurts and negatives and turn then into positives through the process of inner healing. And usually there is pain in the healing process.

When I finally realized that God accepted me just the way I was and had truly forgiven me for the things I had done, I began to enjoy a new freedom. I didn't have to fit into someone else's mold. I could just be me.

I reminded myself of that when Student's Day, the day of the LPN competition, arrived. It was held in Tampa and sponsored by the Licensed Practical Nurses Association. I drove down with several other students from the school.

While the others in the car were chattering away, I was wondering what kind of questions I would be asked at the competition. Would they be technical questions about what we've learned? Personal questions?

I began praying silently, "Lord, if I don't win, it's okay. Just the honor of the nomination is already such a big thing to me. And yet, I know my classmates would like to see our school win. Just help me to give You the glory no matter what happens."

The auditorium seated about a thousand people. There were speeches going on all day and those of us who were there as nominees to compete for the LPN Award had to sit in the back rows of the auditorium. While the program was going on we were pulled out one at a time for our interview.

The President of the LPN Association was speaking when I felt a tap on my shoulder. It was my turn. My nervousness increased as we walked to the conference room.

It was a pleasant, carpeted room and there were

four nurses seated in a row behind a long conference table. They each had a number of folders and papers in front of them.

They stood up as I entered and each one greeted me warmly. Two of them commented on the cheerfulness of my yellow and white uniform. Their friendliness and the small talk helped me to relax.

As I took a seat in front of them, the questioning began.

"Why did you decide to go into nursing?"

"I have a real love for taking care of people. And I think if you really enjoy doing something, then you do it well. Especially if it's also what God wants for your life. I believe that He planted the love and desire within me for nursing. Because I feel it's His will for me, I have been able to make the sacrifices that go along with it."

"What does your husband do for a living?"

"What did you do before you went into nursing?"

"How do you spend your spare time?"

"The law says that a convicted felon cannot be a nurse. What are your feelings on that?"

I told then about the program I was involved with at the women's prison in Lowell and that I had seen Jesus touch many of the inmates' lives. They were now responsible human beings and many of them would make good nurses. I told them I was in favor of changing the law, but that there would have to be a careful screening program for applicants who were ex-felons.

I also shared with them how God changed Frank's life and mine and that God forgives our past. That gives us a clean slate for a new life.

The questions seemed endless. When I finally joined the other students at the back of the auditorium they said, "You're going to win, you've got it!"

"Why do you say that?" I asked.

"Because they kept you in there longer than anyone else."

"Big deal," I said, "I doubt that makes any difference. It just takes me longer to answer questions," I laughed.

At the end of the day all the nominees were called forward and we lined up on the platform. My heart began racing. First came an explanation of the award and what they were looking for in the winner. Then they began talking about the person who won.

When they said, "She's very involved with her community," I relaxed. Well, it's not me, it's someone else. I was actually relieved.

My thoughts drifted off and I was looking out over the audience when I heard the speaker say, "The one thing that really attracted us about her was the gleam in her eye. So -- if Mrs. Cheryl Costantino will come forward . . . "

I froze. Me? Then I saw my teachers and fellow students out in the audience, jumping around; shouting, clapping and hugging each other.

Our school won! I won! I couldn't believe it. Somehow I made it to the podium where I was presented with a plaque and a basket of gifts. Then I was asked if I had anything to say.

"I want to thank my instructors, because they trained me well. They taught me compassion and understanding of the patient as well as the technical things I needed to learn."

"And I want to thank my husband, Frank, who encouraged me to go on and complete what I had begun."

"And thanks to my six kids, who were fairly cooperative through this time."

"But most of all, I want to thank God. So many times I felt like giving up, and He's the one who brought me through all of this."

When the clapping subsided, the meeting was adjourned and I welcomed the hugs and congratulations from teachers and students. As soon as I could break away, I went to a phone and called Frank.

"I won. I'm the LPN of the Year!" I shouted into the phone.

"I knew you were going to win," Frank said. "I told you that you were a winner. I always knew it was in you. Stop by the office on your way home and I'll take you out to dinner." The next day the Sentinel Star read: "The Orange County Vocational School of Practical Nursing has a new feather in its cap. This week, at a state convention, Mrs. Cheryl Costantino was named Practical Student Nurse of the Year, a first for the nursing school. Mrs. Costantino, from St. Cloud, is the mother of six children, ages 3 to 17."

Graduation day was two weeks later. Our friends from church and prayer groups were there. The Bishop wrote to me apologizing that he couldn't make it, but his wife came. Father Al Durrance was there. Many of our relatives were there. The students were justified in all the teasing they gave me about ordering so many graduation tickets. I did have more guests than anyone else.

When the organist began playing "Pomp and Circumstance," I felt like a bride ready to walk down the aisle.

At the end of the program, Miss Newman got up and with a note of pride in her voice said, "A student has won an award for the first time in the history of our school. She competed against all the other schools in the state of Florida. Mrs. Cheryl Costantino is the example of what an LPN is to be in every area of nursing."

The audience gave me a standing ovation as I stood there on the platform, the tears silently sliding down my face. My heart was full of praise to God for taking a loser like me, and making me a winner.

Chapter 15

In just a few hours Frank and I would be flying to San Diego to speak at the Congress of Corrections. Four months had passed since I received the phone call from Rev. Huey Perry. I was looking forward to the trip, but was still nervous about speaking.

Maranatha came running into the kitchen, yelling, "Daddy's home."

As soon as Frank sat down, Maranatha climbed on his lap. She claimed Frank's lap as her spot. She looked quite content with her head against his chest. I smiled as I thought about what a friend of ours had said recently.

"If Bunny ever tells her story, she ought to call it 'The Lion and The Lamb'."

Looking at little Maranatha snuggled up to him, I thought, "Little lamb, you're cuddling with a lion."

"Hey, Mom, want me to load the suitcases in the Pacer for you?" Tony asked.

He had to repack the trunk several times before he could fit everything in Lori's little car. Frank muttered something about taking enough clothes to last six months.

Lori was driving us to the airport and all the kids wanted to ride along, but there just wasn't enough room for eight people. We decided to let the two youngest, Debbie and Maranatha, go along. Michelle was upset that she had to stay home with Tony and Rocco.

When we arrived at our gate at the airport we were told there would be a delay. A problem was discovered and one of the tires had to be changed. When we were finally airborne, the pilot announced over the intercom that we were on a Tri-Star jumbo jet and would be flying at 500 miles per hour at an altitude of 32,000 feet.

Sometimes I felt as if our life was traveling at that speed. But I was thankful that the things we were involved in were worthwhile and changing people's lives. Life in the fast lane was okay when heading in the right direction.

I glanced out my window. The fluffy white clouds looked like cotton candy. I unfastened my seatbelt and settled into the seat. I would enjoy the next few hours of quiet alone with Frank.

The stewardess served our lunch and we pulled down the trays from the seat backs in front of us. Frank prayed, "Bless this food, Oh Lord, and we thank you for it. Feed us now both bodily and spiritually, in Jesus' name. Amen."

I noticed the people across the aisle glancing our way. I guess it was unusual for them to see someone say grace before a meal in a public place. I wondered what they would think if they knew that under that clerical collar of Frank's was a man who spent time in prison. It had been 14 years since he was given that 22 ½ year sentence. Would they believe a man could really change? Ten years ago I wouldn't have believed it myself.

The plane touched down in San Diego and we took a cab to the Hanalei Hotel, where reservations had been made for us. Statues of ancient Hawaiian gods, potted palms, and thatched roofs created a beautiful Polynesian atmosphere.

Our room was on the second floor. It had two queen-sized beds, color T.V., and a separate lounge. Sliding glass doors opened onto a balcony with wrought-iron furniture. Looking out from the balcony we could see a mountain in the distance. Directly below the balcony was a Polynesian hut, exotic plants and trees, and a waterfall. It was beautiful and I was glad I had accepted the invitation to speak.

The next morning Chaplain Ray Hoekstra of International Prison Ministry and his wife, Leola, picked us up for breakfast. Then we drove to the convention center where the Congress of Corrections was held.

We roamed around, looking at the displays and literature tables different groups had set up. When it was time for us to speak, we were ushered to a head table set up in front of an assembly hall. There were to be four speakers, each speaking for about 15 minutes. I unfolded the prepared speech I had written out and fidgeted nervously with the pages.

A representative from the Salvation Army spoke first, then someone who ran a half-way house for released prisoners. I was relieved when they introduced Frank next.

The master of ceremonies said, "I know it's usually 'ladies before gentlemen,' but today we're going to reverse that."

It gave me another 15 minutes to look over my notes. The applause at the close of Frank's speech made me even more nervous. The master of ceremonies stood, made a few introductory remarks, and then said, "And now, here's Mrs. Cheryl Costantino."

As I walked over to the podium I tried to appear calm, but my whole body was shaking inside. I placed my notes on the podium, and gripped the sides of the lectern with both hands.

As I looked up and out at the audience, it slowly dawned on me that these were the people that I once considered to be my enemies – – policemen, lawyers, prosecuters, anyone involved in corrections.

As I was about to begin, there was some distraction at the rear of the auditorium, and the master of ceremonies motioned for me to wait. The clanging of folding chairs could be heard, as extra rows were being set up to accomodate the overflow crowd. There was an air of anticipation as everyone settled down and I began my speech.

"As an inmate's wife, I found life to be very difficult," I said. My voice came out in a higher-than-normal pitch. I tried clearing my throat, but it didn't help much.

"I discovered how cruel people could be – people that would not have been cruel, and weren't, when my husband was home.

"Men talk down to a woman who doesn't have a husband to back her up. I was to learn that over and over again in the four years that my husband was gone. It's amazing how quickly men move in on a woman when they find out that her husband has been sent to prison. Not necessarily sexually, although there is some of that.

"They move in to pick the carcass of a broken home or family – to make a quick cash deal on a car if a woman needs a lawyer or money; or a possible house repossession if she can't keep up the payments with the head of the house gone. The people that owed us money, and even our friends, didn't come by because they were afraid that I would ask for five dollars for food.

"People were cruel to my children. It's hard to imagine adults picking on and heckling children because their father is a 'jailbird', but they did and I had a hard time dealing with that.

"I was harassed by the police, because they hated my husband. Once he was in prison where they could no longer harass him, they started in on me. They stopped me every time that I got into my car to go somewhere, and told me that they wouldn't be happy until I was in prison, too. They would stop the only friends that bothered to come by and tell them that if they entered my house they would be arrested. And my friends were straight people who worked legitimate jobs. They certainly didn't want to be arrested."

I looked up from my notes into the sea of faces and could tell they were really listening. My hands loosened their tight grip on the podium and my body and voice relaxed. They seemed genuinely interested in what I was saying.

"I also had to face the first shock of living alone. I was frightened at night and couldn't sleep. Things looked very dark for me at that time. Frank was in Raiford, 300 miles away, with a 22 ½ year prison sentence. The Parole Board sent me a letter saying his parole date was in 11 years. I didn't know anything about prison life or parole; this was my first experience.

"I questioned whether or not I wanted to wait eleven years for Frank to come home. I was only 22 years old, and eleven years was a long time to be alone. What if I waited and he came home, only to return to prison a month or two later? Did I want to take that chance? What a waste of life for me and my children. I was very confused and my life lacked direction. I loved Frank, but I didn't know if I loved him enough to make that kind of sacrifice.

"I had never been a drinker, but after Frank was gone for about a year, I started drinking quite heavily. I couldn't cope with the financial pressures that I was under, in addition to the other pressures that were pouring in on me from all sides. My world seemed to be falling apart around me and I wondered why I was made to suffer for what Frank did. At that time, I was well into the nervous breakdown that I would experience just a few months later.

"I'm quite sure that judges do not realize that when they sentence a man to prison, they sentence his family with him.

"The initial state is quite traumatic. It's not only a family separated, a breadwinner gone, financial collapse, or fear of being alone, as if all that were not enough. It's the pressure of being a social outcast, the wife of a prisoner, with children not wanting to play with your children, or saying mean or hateful things as kids can do.

"Police pressure, and pressure from friends, all mix in with the absence of hope. It was the combination of these things that made me want to drop out. I was filled with many different feelings at that time – all of which were negative. Fear, hate, loneliness, frustration, confusion, anxiety, depression and many more emotions flooded me.

"It's really hard to say what my feelings towards Frank were. When pressures would let up a little, I loved him. When the electricity was shut off, or my kids hadn't eaten in three days, I hated him.

"There were days when all that my children had to eat was a piece of toast. There weren't any food stamps in Florida at that time, and the little that welfare gave didn't pay the bills and buy food. I didn't have a trade, and working for minimum wage is a waste of time when you have four children under the age of seven. Babysitters ate up a paycheck, and welfare would stop their aid if you worked, so you couldn't win for losing. So, sometimes I missed Frank and wanted him home, and at other times I hated him for the pain I was experiencing.

"I always felt as if I were a third wheel. I didn't fit socially. I was married, but I didn't have a husband at home, and I didn't fit in with single people because I was married.

"Women whose husbands are in prison generally have a very low self-image. They lose their self-respect. I felt as though I were useless, an outcast, stamped with the stigma of that prison sentence. There is a certain amount of paranoia attached to this kind of life. I really had the feeling that everybody knew what my situation was and where my husband was. That sense of low esteem was only accented by visits to the county jail or to the prison.

"After Frank had been in prison two years or so, a chaplain there prayed with him for his salvation. A year later I accepted Christ. With Christ came the hope that was missing from my life."

A burst of applause interrupted me. The Christians in the audience understood and agreed with what I was saying. They knew the reality of a changed life through Jesus. When the applause died down, I continued.

"I would stress the fact that anyone who is working with the families of prisoners must be sensitive to the feeling of hopelessness that can sometimes take over the mind. Jesus Christ, who is the Source of hope, MUST be shared. It's important to be sensitive to the social and spiritual needs of the prison family, as well as the inmates.

"Ideally, Christian fellowship has the potential to be the support group that can absorb the needs of the prisoner's family. The fact that all were lost, but now are found, makes an outcast feel as though he is joined with others who were outcasts.

"I say 'ideally' because although most Christians confess that we are all the same before God, in practice this does not always apply to their manner of living.

"I didn't feel a part of the first fellowship I went to after I accepted Christ, while my husband was still in prison. Other Christian women did not want their husbands doing anything for me, and I felt like a charity case even though I hadn't asked for anything. In spite of that, I could see that the way Jesus wanted me to live was the right way, and my hope rested in the fact that He was still working on all of us.

"After Frank came home there were a lot of adjustments that had to be made. Our oldest daughter suffered the most, because she was old enough to understand some of what was happening during the prison experience. She was filled with a lot of hate and resentment, but three years ago she accepted Christ, and gave all of that hate to Him. All of my children are now Christians, and they are very proud of their dad and the work that he is doing, and so am I. Only Christ could restore the years that were wasted.

"It took me nine years to fully regain my self-worth. I returned to school, got my highschool diploma, went on to nursing school, and graduated last May. I was chosen Student LPN of the Year for the state of Florida, and received the Health Occupation Award for outstanding student leadership and achievement. Only God can take a loser and turn her into a winner."

The applause kept building as I gathered my notes and went back to my seat at the head table. Frank leaned over and said, "You did good, baby."

As I listened to the applause, I realized that what I had said had an impact on the audience. The same criminal justice people that I at one time hated, were now responding to what I had to say to them.

The master of ceremonies held up his hand for quiet and announced that there would now be a thirty minute question and answer period. Those in the audience could ask any one of us questions in response to what we spoke on.

Many hands shot up at once and most of the questions were directed to me. I could tell by their probing that the people were really searching for answers and wrestling with how best to help the families of inmates.

A parole commissioner asked, "How do you feel about conjugal visits?" In reply I said, "I think conjugal visits would help cut down on the problem of homosexuality in the prisons. That occasional privacy between husband and wife is one of the important factors that could help keep a family together."

A lady from New Jersey asked, "Have you written a book about your experiences?"

"No," I smiled, "I haven't."

"Well, I hope you will consider doing it," she replied.

A parole officer asked, "What kinds of things could be done to help hold the family together while in prison?"

I injected a little humor and suggested they consider building family cells. Three bedrooms, two baths. The family that does time together, stays together."

That drew a round of laughter.

One man stood and asked, "To what do you and Frank really attribute being able to make it?"

"As Frank already shared with you," I said, "Rehabilitation didn't work. Regeneration works. Jesus works."

Many of the chaplains responded with their "Amens."

Another man stood and said, "I never stopped to think before about what an inmate's wife goes through. You've really touched me today and I want to thank you for coming."

That drew another round of applause and then the master of ceremonies said the thirty minutes were up and dismissed the meeting.

Huey Perry excitedly made his way over to me and gave me a big hug. "Thank you, Bunny. That was great! Do you realize there were more people at this workshop than at any of the others in the whole Congress? We had to keep bringing in extra chairs. And I know what you said was well received."

He was interrupted by someone from the Salvation Army.

"I'm so glad you shared your faith in God and that He's the one who changed your life," he said.

I told him that the work the Salvation Army was doing with inmate families around the country was good and that I was convinced it was because they, too, brought God into their program and their counseling.

One by one people made their way through the crowd and came over to me, all wanting to talk at the same time, expressing their appreciation of helping them to understand what the wife of an inmate goes through.

I felt overwhelmed by the response and excitement as I realized that they *cared*. I never thought these people really cared. But I knew then that they *did!*

Epilogue

Chaplain Ray and his wife Leola invited Frank and Bunny out for dinner when the Congress was over and the four of them sat around the table discussing the day's events.

"Well, Bunny," Chaplain Ray said, "How did your speech go? I'm afraid I got tied up with my book display and didn't make it to hear you."

"Quite honestly, I wasn't convinced that my sharing with them would really make any difference," Bunny answered.

"But it has," Leola said. "People listened and were moved by what you said."

"You know," Leola said to Chaplain Ray, "the women really haven't had much attention. All the programs have been focused on the inmate and there's almost nothing for their families. I think the time has come for a story like Bunny's to be told."

"You know, Champ," Chaplain Ray said to Frank, "we really ought to consider doing that. Maybe God is speaking to us through all of this. Perhaps the time has come for us to take a closer look at the needs of the inmate families."

"How do you feel about writing your story, Bunny?" Chaplain Ray asked.

"Do you really think the story of my life could help

another prisoner's wife during her hard time? What about the failures I had?''

"A person may fail many times, but he or she is not a failure until they start blaming someone else. You have found the way to overcome your problems, and that is the story that needs to be told to prisoners' wives everywhere."

Bunny's eyes filled with tears as she shared the Bible passage she had read that morning from Isaiah 51:16. *"I have put my words in thy mouth, and I have covered thee in the shadow of mine hand . . . "* (K.J.V.)

THE END